Effective Public Speaking

A Practical Guide for Confident Communication

Park Windsor

Contents

Chapter 1
The Power of Public Speaking

Understanding the Impact of Effective Communication

Effective communication is a cornerstone of success in both personal and professional realms. Public speaking, in particular, is a powerful tool for conveying ideas, influencing others, and building relationships. Understanding the impact of effective communication can help individuals harness its power to achieve their goals.

1. **Inspiration and Motivation:** A skilled public speaker has the ability to inspire and motivate their audience. Through compelling storytelling, engaging anecdotes, and passionate delivery, they can ignite enthusiasm and drive action in others. By tapping into the emotions of their listeners, effective communicators can spur individuals or groups to pursue their goals with renewed vigor.

2. **Influence and Persuasion:** Public speaking enables individuals to articulate their ideas persuasively, thereby influencing the thoughts, beliefs, and behaviors of others. Whether delivering a sales pitch, advocating for a cause, or seeking support for a project, persuasive communication skills are invaluable. By crafting persuasive arguments and presenting them with confidence and conviction, speakers can sway opinions and garner support for their initiatives.

3. **Building Trust and Credibility:** Trust is the foundation of any meaningful relationship, whether in business, politics, or personal life. Effective public speaking fosters trust by establishing credibility and authenticity. When speakers demonstrate expertise, sincerity, and integrity, they earn the trust of their audience. Moreover, by communicating with clarity and transparency, speakers cultivate an atmosphere of openness and honesty, further strengthening trust-based relationships.

4. **Fostering Connection and Understanding:** Public speaking facilitates meaningful connections between speakers and their audience. Through empathetic communication, speakers can relate to the experiences, concerns, and aspirations of their listeners, fostering a sense of camaraderie and solidarity. By sharing personal anecdotes, acknowledging common challenges, and offering practical insights,

speakers can bridge divides and cultivate a sense of understanding and unity among diverse audiences.

5. **Empowerment and Self-Confidence:** Finally, effective public speaking empowers individuals to express themselves confidently and assertively. By mastering the art of communication, individuals can overcome self-doubt, conquer stage fright, and project an aura of self-assurance. As they hone their speaking skills and witness the positive impact of their words on others, speakers experience a boost in self-confidence and self-esteem, empowering them to tackle new challenges and seize opportunities with gusto.

Overcoming Fear and Nervousness

Overcoming fear and nervousness is a crucial aspect of mastering public speaking and harnessing its power effectively. Here's a practical guide to help individuals conquer stage fright and speak with confidence:

1. **Prepare Thoroughly:** The more prepared you are, the less nervous you'll feel. Familiarize yourself with your topic, organize your thoughts, and create a clear outline or script for your speech. Practice delivering your presentation multiple times until you feel comfortable with the material. Rehearsing in front of a mirror or recording yourself can also help build confidence.

2. **Know Your Audience:** Understanding your audience can alleviate anxiety by making you feel more connected to them. Research their demographics, interests, and preferences to tailor your message accordingly. Knowing that you're speaking to individuals who are receptive to your message can boost your confidence and ease nervousness.

3. **Visualize Success:** Visualization is a powerful technique for reducing anxiety and boosting confidence. Close your eyes and imagine yourself delivering your speech with poise and confidence. Visualize the audience responding positively to your words and gestures. This mental rehearsal can help reframe your mindset from one of fear to one of success.

4. **Practice Relaxation Techniques:** Incorporate relaxation techniques into your pre-speech routine to calm your nerves. Deep breathing exercises, progressive muscle relaxation, or meditation can help alleviate physical tension and promote a sense of calmness. Practice these techniques before your speech and during any moments of anxiety on stage.

5. **Focus on the Message, Not Yourself:** Shift your focus away from yourself and onto your message and audience. Remind yourself that you're there to share valuable information, inspire, or entertain—not to impress or be judged. Concentrate on the importance of your message and how it can benefit your audience. This shift in focus can reduce self-consciousness and nervousness.

6. **Start Small:** If you're new to public speaking or experiencing intense fear, start with smaller speaking engagements or practice sessions. Join a public speaking club, where you can gradually build your skills in a supportive environment. As you gain experience and confidence, gradually take on larger speaking opportunities.

7. **Embrace Imperfection:** Accept that it's natural to feel nervous before speaking in public, and that occasional mistakes are inevitable. Instead of striving for perfection, focus on being authentic and connecting with your audience. Embrace any imperfections or mistakes as part of the learning process, and use them as opportunities for growth.

8. **Seek Support:** Don't be afraid to seek support from friends, mentors, or a professional coach to help you overcome your fear of public speaking. Share your concerns with someone you trust, and ask for constructive feedback and encouragement. Having a supportive network can provide reassurance and motivation as you work towards becoming a more confident speaker.

The Role of Public Speaking in Personal and Professional Growth

Public speaking plays a pivotal role in both personal and professional growth, offering numerous benefits that extend beyond mere communication skills. Here's a breakdown of how public speaking contributes to personal and professional development:

1. Communication Skills Enhancement: Public speaking is a masterclass in communication. It teaches individuals how to articulate their thoughts clearly, concisely, and persuasively. Through the process of crafting speeches, delivering presentations, and engaging with diverse audiences, speakers refine their verbal and non-verbal communication skills, including tone, body language, and vocal delivery. These enhanced communication skills are invaluable in personal relationships, professional settings, and everyday interactions.

2. Confidence Building: Public speaking is one of the most effective ways to build self-confidence. Facing an audience and delivering a speech requires individuals to step outside their comfort zone, confront their fears, and project confidence and competence. As speakers gain experience and receive positive feedback, they develop a sense of self-assurance that extends beyond the stage. This newfound confidence empowers individuals to tackle challenges, seize opportunities, and assert themselves in various aspects of their lives.

3. Leadership Development: Effective public speaking is closely linked to leadership skills development. Leaders must be able to inspire, influence, and motivate others through their words and actions. By mastering the art of public speaking, individuals cultivate the qualities of a strong leader, including vision, charisma, and the ability to inspire trust and confidence in others. Whether leading a team, managing projects, or driving organizational change, strong communication skills are essential for effective leadership.

4. Networking Opportunities: Public speaking provides individuals with valuable networking opportunities that can accelerate personal and professional growth. Speaking at conferences, seminars, or industry events allows individuals to showcase their expertise, establish credibility, and connect with like-minded professionals. Networking through public speaking enables individuals to expand their professional network, forge meaningful relationships, and uncover new career opportunities.

5. Personal Branding: Public speaking is a powerful tool for building and promoting a personal brand. By consistently delivering compelling speeches on topics of expertise, individuals can position themselves as thought leaders and subject matter experts in their field. Public speaking engagements enhance visibility, credibility, and recognition within professional circles, elevating individuals' personal brands and opening doors to career advancement and opportunities for collaboration.

6. Continuous Learning and Growth: Public speaking is a journey of continuous learning and growth. Each speaking opportunity provides individuals with the chance to refine their skills, learn from feedback, and evolve as communicators. Whether experimenting with new presentation techniques, exploring different speaking styles, or honing storytelling abilities, speakers are constantly challenging themselves to improve and innovate. This commitment to lifelong learning fosters personal and professional growth, enabling individuals to stay relevant, adaptable, and resilient in an ever-changing world.

The Connection Between Confidence and Public Speaking

The connection between confidence and public speaking is profound and mutually reinforcing. Confidence is not only a prerequisite for effective public speaking but also a natural byproduct of mastering this skill. Here's a breakdown of the relationship between confidence and public speaking:

1. Confidence Enables Effective Communication: Confidence is essential for effective public speaking because it enables speakers to communicate their message with clarity, conviction, and authority. When speakers believe in themselves and their message, they convey confidence through their words, tone of voice, and body language. This confidence captivates the audience's attention, fosters trust, and enhances the speaker's persuasive impact.

2. Preparation Breeds Confidence: One of the keys to confidence in public speaking is thorough preparation. When speakers invest time and effort in researching their topic, organizing their thoughts, and practicing their delivery, they feel more confident in their ability to deliver a compelling presentation. Preparation instills a sense of mastery and readiness, alleviating anxiety and bolstering confidence on stage.

3. Experience Builds Confidence: Confidence in public speaking grows with experience. As speakers gain exposure to different speaking opportunities, they become more familiar with the dynamics of public speaking and develop greater self-assurance. Each successful speaking engagement reinforces their confidence, while setbacks provide valuable learning experiences that contribute to their growth as speakers.

4. Positive Feedback Reinforces Confidence: Positive feedback from audience members, peers, or mentors can significantly boost a speaker's confidence. When speakers receive praise for their presentation skills, content, or delivery, it validates their efforts and reinforces their belief in their abilities. This positive reinforcement bolsters confidence and motivates speakers to continue honing their public speaking skills.

5. Mindset Matters: Confidence in public speaking is also influenced by mindset. Adopting a positive and optimistic mindset can help speakers overcome self-doubt, fear of failure, and negative self-talk. By reframing challenges as opportunities for growth, visualizing success, and focusing on their strengths, speakers can cultivate a resilient mindset that fuels confidence in public speaking.

6. Confidence Begets Success: Confidence in public speaking creates a virtuous cycle of success. As speakers exude confidence on stage, they engage their audience more effectively, convey authority and credibility, and increase the likelihood of achieving their communication goals. This success, in turn, reinforces their confidence, motivating them to tackle more ambitious speaking opportunities and continue their journey of growth and development.

7. Continuous Improvement: Confidence in public speaking is not static but dynamic, evolving over time through continuous learning and improvement. Even the most seasoned speakers experience moments of nervousness or self-doubt, but they have learned to manage these feelings and channel them into positive energy. By embracing a growth mindset, seeking feedback, and persistently striving for improvement, speakers can cultivate unwavering confidence in their public speaking abilities.

Setting Clear Communication Goals

Setting clear communication goals is essential for effective public speaking. These goals provide a roadmap for crafting your message, engaging your audience, and achieving your desired outcomes. Here's how to set clear communication goals for your public speaking endeavors:

1. **Define Your Purpose:** Begin by clarifying the purpose of your speech. Ask yourself: What do I hope to accomplish with this presentation? Are you aiming to inform, persuade, inspire, entertain, or educate your audience? Defining your purpose will guide the content, structure, and tone of your speech.

2. **Identify Your Audience:** Consider who your audience is and what they want or need to hear. Are they experts in your field, novices, or a mixed group? What are their interests, concerns, and preferences? Tailor your message to resonate with your audience's demographics, values, and expectations.

3. **Determine Key Messages:** Identify the key messages you want to convey during your speech. These are the main ideas or takeaways that you want your audience to remember. Keep your messages clear, concise, and relevant to your audience's needs and interests.

4. **Set Specific Objectives:** Establish specific objectives or outcomes that you want to achieve through your speech. These could include raising awareness about a particular issue, influencing opinions,

motivating action, or fostering understanding. Make sure your objectives are measurable, achievable, and aligned with your overall purpose.

5. **Craft a Compelling Narrative:** Structure your speech around a compelling narrative that engages your audience from beginning to end. Start with a strong opening that grabs attention, followed by a clear introduction of your main points, supporting evidence or examples, and a memorable conclusion that reinforces your key messages.

6. **Consider Timing and Logistics:** Factor in logistical considerations such as the time allotted for your speech, the venue, audiovisual equipment, and any other practicalities. Plan your content and delivery accordingly to ensure that you stay within the time constraints and make the most of the available resources.

7. **Adapt to Feedback and Evaluation:** Be open to feedback and evaluation from others, both before and after your speech. Solicit input from peers, mentors, or trusted advisors to help you refine your message, delivery, and overall effectiveness. Use feedback to iterate and improve your public speaking skills over time.

8. **Practice and Rehearse:** Practice is essential for achieving your communication goals. Rehearse your speech multiple times, focusing on delivery, timing, and expression. Use techniques such as visualization, role-playing, or recording yourself to fine-tune your performance and build confidence.

Chapter 2
Crafting Compelling Content

Structuring Your Speech: Introduction, Body, Conclusion

Structuring your speech effectively is crucial for engaging your audience, conveying your message clearly, and leaving a lasting impression. Here's a guide to structuring your speech into three key components: the introduction, body, and conclusion:

1. Introduction:

a. Attention Grabber: Begin your speech with a strong attention-grabbing opening that captures the audience's interest and draws them in. This could be a compelling story, a shocking statistic, a thought-provoking question, or a powerful quote related to your topic.

b. Relevance Statement: After grabbing attention, provide a brief overview of why your topic is relevant and important to your audience. Highlight the significance of your message and how it relates to their interests, concerns, or aspirations. This helps establish a connection with your audience and sets the context for your speech.

c. Thesis Statement: Clearly state the main purpose or thesis of your speech. This should succinctly outline the central idea or argument you will be presenting throughout the speech. Your thesis statement acts as a roadmap for the audience, guiding them through the key points you will address in the body of your speech.

2. Body:

a. Main Points: The body of your speech should consist of several main points that support and develop your thesis statement. Organize your main points logically, grouping related ideas together and presenting them in a coherent sequence. Each main point should be distinct, relevant, and supported by evidence, examples, or anecdotes.

b. Supporting Evidence: Provide supporting evidence or examples to substantiate your main points and enhance their credibility. Use a variety of sources such as research findings, statistics, expert opinions, personal experiences, or real-life stories to illustrate your arguments and make them more compelling.

c. Transitions: Use transitions to smoothly navigate between different main points and maintain the flow of your speech. Transitional phrases or sentences help signal shifts in topics or ideas, reinforce connections between points, and keep the audience engaged. Examples of transitions include "now that we've discussed...", "moving on to our next point...", or "in addition to..."

3. Conclusion:

a. Recap: Summarize the main points you covered in the body of your speech. Reinforce your thesis statement by reminding the audience of the key ideas you presented and the significance of your message.

b. Closing Statement: End your speech with a memorable closing statement that leaves a lasting impression on your audience. This could be a call to action, a thought-provoking question, a memorable quote, or a powerful closing thought that reinforces the main takeaway of your speech.

c. Closure: Provide a sense of closure by signaling that your speech is coming to an end. Use phrases such as "in conclusion," "to wrap up," or "to summarize" to indicate that you are wrapping up your remarks and preparing to conclude.

Capturing Audience Attention from the Start

Capturing audience attention from the start is essential for engaging your listeners and setting the tone for your speech. Here are some effective strategies to captivate your audience right from the beginning:

1. **Start with a Story:** Open your speech with a captivating story that resonates with your audience and relates to your topic. Stories have a unique ability to evoke emotions, pique curiosity, and draw listeners

in. Choose a narrative that is relevant, relatable, and compelling, and use vivid details to paint a vivid picture in the minds of your audience.

2. **Pose a Provocative Question:** Begin with a thought-provoking question that stimulates curiosity and encourages active engagement from your audience. Pose a question that challenges conventional thinking, sparks debate, or prompts reflection. This encourages listeners to mentally engage with your topic and sets the stage for the discussion to follow.

3. **Use Startling Statistics or Facts:** Capture attention by presenting surprising or startling statistics or facts related to your topic. Choose data that is relevant, credible, and unexpected, and present it in a way that grabs the audience's attention immediately. Shocking statistics or compelling facts can jolt listeners out of complacency and create a sense of urgency or importance around your message.

4. **Employ a Powerful Quote:** Open with a powerful quote that encapsulates the essence of your message or highlights a key theme of your speech. Select a quote from a respected authority, a well-known figure, or a relevant source, and use it to add credibility and resonance to your opening remarks. A compelling quote can inspire, provoke thought, or evoke emotion, capturing the audience's attention and setting a tone for your speech.

5. **Create a Visual Image:** Paint a visual image in the minds of your audience by using descriptive language or vivid imagery. Describe a scene, a scenario, or an anecdote that transports listeners to a specific time and place, engaging their imagination and drawing them into your story. Visual language can create a sense of immediacy and captivate the audience's attention from the start.

6. **Utilize Humor:** Begin with a light-hearted joke, anecdote, or humorous observation to break the ice and establish rapport with your audience. Humor has the power to put listeners at ease, build connections, and create a positive atmosphere conducive to engagement and receptivity. Just ensure that your humor is appropriate for the context and audience, and aligns with the tone of your speech.

7. **Invoke Emotion:** Appeal to the emotions of your audience by tapping into their hopes, fears, desires, or aspirations. Start with a heartfelt personal story, an emotional anecdote, or a poignant observation that resonates with listeners on an emotional level. Emotionally charged content can capture attention, foster empathy, and create a powerful connection between you and your audience.

8. **Use Multimedia or Props:** Incorporate multimedia elements such as videos, images, or props into your opening to add visual interest and enhance engagement. Show a compelling video clip, display striking visuals, or introduce a relevant prop that captures attention and reinforces your message. Multimedia can add depth and dynamism to your opening, making it more memorable and impactful.

Crafting a Clear and Memorable Message

Crafting a clear and memorable message is essential for effective public speaking. Your message serves as the foundation of your speech, guiding the content, structure, and delivery. Here are steps to help you craft a message that resonates with your audience:

1. **Define Your Core Idea:** Start by defining the core idea or main point you want to convey in your speech. This is the central theme or takeaway that you want your audience to remember long after your presentation is over. Your core idea should be clear, concise, and relevant to your audience's interests and needs.

2. **Focus on Key Takeaways:** Identify the key takeaways or main points that support your core idea. These are the most important pieces of information or insights that you want your audience to understand and remember. Limit yourself to a few key takeaways to avoid overwhelming your audience with too much information.

3. **Structure Your Message:** Organize your message in a logical and coherent structure that guides the flow of your speech. Start with an attention-grabbing introduction that introduces your core idea and previews the main points you will cover. Then, develop your main

points in the body of your speech, providing supporting evidence, examples, or anecdotes to reinforce each point. Finally, conclude your speech by summarizing your key takeaways and reinforcing your core idea.

4. **Use Clear and Concise Language:** Communicate your message using clear, concise language that is easy for your audience to understand. Avoid jargon, technical terms, or complex language that may confuse or alienate your audience. Instead, use simple, straightforward language that resonates with your audience and effectively conveys your message.

5. **Employ Vivid Imagery and Storytelling:** Enhance your message with vivid imagery and storytelling techniques that bring your ideas to life and make them more memorable. Use descriptive language, sensory details, and engaging anecdotes to create a mental picture in the minds of your audience. Stories have a unique ability to captivate attention, evoke emotions, and illustrate complex ideas in a relatable way.

6. **Reinforce Your Message Throughout:** Consistently reinforce your core idea and key takeaways throughout your speech to ensure that they resonate with your audience. Repetition is key to memory retention, so find creative ways to reiterate your message without sounding redundant. Use rhetorical devices such as parallelism, alliteration, or rhetorical questions to reinforce key points and keep your audience engaged.

7. **Craft a Memorable Closing:** End your speech with a memorable closing that leaves a lasting impression on your audience. Summarize your key takeaways, restate your core idea, and leave your audience with a thought-provoking question, a call to action, or a powerful closing statement that reinforces the significance of your message.

8. **Practice and Refine:** Practice delivering your speech multiple times to ensure that your message is clear, concise, and impactful. Pay attention to your pacing, tone, and delivery, and make adjustments as needed to enhance clarity and effectiveness. Solicit feedback from

peers, mentors, or trusted advisors to identify areas for improvement and refine your message until it resonates with your audience.

Developing Engaging Stories and Examples

Developing engaging stories and examples is a powerful way to enrich your public speaking content, capture your audience's attention, and make your message more memorable. Here's a guide to help you craft compelling stories and examples for your speeches:

1. **Start with Relevance:** Choose stories and examples that are relevant to your audience and directly support your main points. Consider their interests, experiences, and concerns, and select anecdotes that resonate with them on a personal level. Relevance is key to maintaining audience engagement and ensuring that your stories have a meaningful impact.

2. **Create Emotional Connection:** Aim to create an emotional connection with your audience through your stories and examples. Tap into universal emotions such as joy, sadness, fear, or hope to evoke empathy and engagement. Share personal anecdotes, real-life experiences, or powerful testimonials that stir emotions and make your message more relatable and memorable.

3. **Show, Don't Just Tell:** Use vivid imagery and descriptive language to paint a vivid picture in the minds of your audience. Instead of simply describing events or situations, show them through sensory details, dialogue, and scene-setting. Transport your audience to the moment of your story and immerse them in the experience, making it more vivid and impactful.

4. **Keep it Concise and Relevant:** Be mindful of the length and relevance of your stories and examples. Keep them concise and focused on the key message or takeaway you want to convey. Avoid tangents or unnecessary details that detract from the main point of your speech. Every story or example should directly contribute to your overall message and reinforce your main points.

5. **Add Humor and Anecdotes:** Inject humor and lighthearted anecdotes into your stories to keep your audience engaged and entertained. Humor can break the ice, alleviate tension, and make your message more memorable. Share amusing anecdotes, funny incidents, or relatable observations that add a touch of levity to your speech and connect with your audience on a human level.

6. **Provide Concrete Examples:** Use concrete, tangible examples to illustrate abstract concepts and make your ideas more tangible and understandable. Provide real-life examples, case studies, or success stories that demonstrate the practical application of your ideas and show their relevance in the real world. Concrete examples help clarify complex concepts and make them more accessible to your audience.

7. **Create Dramatic Tension:** Introduce dramatic tension or conflict into your stories to heighten interest and keep your audience hooked. Highlight challenges, obstacles, or dilemmas that characters face, and build suspense as you lead up to the resolution. Dramatic tension creates anticipation and keeps your audience engaged as they eagerly await the outcome of the story.

8. **End with a Resolution or Lesson:** Conclude your stories and examples with a clear resolution or takeaway that reinforces your main message. Reflect on the lessons learned, insights gained, or changes experienced as a result of the story. End on a positive note that leaves your audience feeling inspired, enlightened, or motivated to take action based on the story you've shared.

Tailoring Content to Your Audience

Tailoring your content to your audience is essential for effective public speaking. Understanding your audience's demographics, interests, needs, and preferences allows you to create content that resonates with them on a deeper level. Here's how to tailor your content to your audience:

1. **Know Your Audience:** Conduct thorough research to understand who your audience is. Consider factors such as their age, gender,

occupation, education level, cultural background, and familiarity with the topic. Gather insights through surveys, interviews, or observations to gain a deeper understanding of their preferences, interests, and expectations.

2. **Identify Their Needs and Concerns:** Put yourself in your audience's shoes and consider what they hope to gain from your speech. Identify their needs, concerns, challenges, and aspirations, and tailor your content to address these effectively. Offer solutions, insights, or guidance that directly speak to their interests and concerns, demonstrating that you understand and empathize with their perspective.

3. **Adapt Your Language and Tone:** Use language and tone that resonates with your audience and matches their level of knowledge and expertise. Avoid jargon, technical terms, or industry-specific language that may be unfamiliar or alienating to your audience. Instead, use clear, accessible language that is easy to understand and relevant to their experiences.

4. **Highlight Relevant Examples and Stories:** Incorporate examples, anecdotes, and stories that are relevant and relatable to your audience's experiences and interests. Choose examples that illustrate key concepts or ideas in a way that resonates with their lives, challenges, or aspirations. Personalize your examples to make them more compelling and memorable for your audience.

5. **Address Their Interests and Preferences:** Tailor your content to align with your audience's interests, hobbies, and preferences. Consider what topics or themes are most likely to captivate their attention and keep them engaged throughout your speech. Customize your content to reflect their interests and passions, making it more relevant and appealing to them.

6. **Acknowledge Their Prior Knowledge:** Recognize the level of familiarity and expertise your audience has with the topic and adjust your content accordingly. Avoid overwhelming beginners with too much technical detail or boring experts with basic information they already

know. Strike the right balance by offering insights and information that are appropriate for your audience's level of knowledge and expertise.

7. Address Their Motivations and Goals: Consider what motivates your audience and what goals they hope to achieve by listening to your speech. Tailor your content to speak to their motivations, aspirations, and desires, offering insights or inspiration that resonate with their personal or professional goals. Show them how your message can help them overcome challenges, achieve success, or realize their dreams.

8. Invite Audience Interaction and Participation: Foster engagement and interaction by inviting audience members to participate in your speech. Ask questions, encourage discussion, or incorporate interactive elements such as polls, Q&A sessions, or group activities. By involving your audience directly, you create a more dynamic and engaging experience that keeps them actively involved and invested in your message.

Chapter 3
Mastering Non-Verbal Communication

The Importance of Body Language

Body language is a critical component of effective public speaking, as it can significantly impact how your message is perceived and received by your audience. Here's why body language is important in public speaking:

1. **Conveys Confidence and Authority:** Your body language communicates volumes about your confidence and authority as a speaker. Standing tall, maintaining eye contact, and using open gestures convey confidence and assertiveness, while slouching, avoiding eye contact, or fidgeting can signal nervousness or insecurity. Projecting confidence through your body language enhances your credibility and persuasiveness as a speaker.

2. **Enhances Engagement and Connection:** Engaging body language helps captivate your audience's attention and fosters a stronger connection with them. Smiling, nodding, and making appropriate facial expressions demonstrate warmth and empathy, inviting your audience to connect with you on a personal level. Using expressive gestures, such as hand movements or facial expressions, can also help reinforce key points and keep your audience engaged throughout your speech.

3. **Reinforces Verbal Messages:** Your body language acts as a powerful amplifier for your verbal messages, reinforcing and emphasizing key points in your speech. For example, using hand gestures to illustrate size or shape, nodding to affirm agreement, or leaning forward to show interest can enhance the impact of your words and make your message more memorable. Aligning your verbal and non-verbal communication creates a cohesive and compelling presentation that resonates with your audience.

4. **Communicates Emotions and Energy:** Body language allows you to convey emotions and energy levels that words alone cannot express. Expressive facial expressions, vocal inflections, and body movements can convey enthusiasm, passion, excitement, or urgency, creating an emotional connection with your audience and eliciting a corresponding response. By harnessing the power of non-verbal communication, you

can evoke emotions, inspire action, and leave a lasting impression on your audience.

5. Facilitates Understanding and Comprehension: Clear and effective body language can enhance understanding and comprehension of your message, especially for visual or kinesthetic learners. Using visual aids, such as gestures, props, or visual cues, can help clarify complex concepts, illustrate abstract ideas, and enhance memory retention. By incorporating visual elements into your presentation, you make your message more accessible and easier to understand for diverse audience members.

6. Manages Audience Dynamics: Body language can be used to manage audience dynamics and maintain control over the speaking environment. For example, making eye contact with individuals throughout the audience can help keep them engaged and attentive, while adjusting your body position or movement can signal transitions or changes in focus. By monitoring audience reactions and adjusting your body language accordingly, you can effectively navigate the speaking situation and ensure that your message is received as intended.

Using Gestures and Facial Expressions Effectively

Using gestures and facial expressions effectively is essential for enhancing your non-verbal communication skills and engaging your audience during public speaking. Here's how to leverage gestures and facial expressions to maximize the impact of your message:

1. Understand Cultural Context: Be mindful of cultural differences in gestures and facial expressions, as what may be appropriate or meaningful in one culture could be misunderstood or offensive in another. Research cultural norms and customs if you're speaking to an audience from diverse cultural backgrounds, and adapt your gestures and expressions accordingly to ensure inclusivity and respect.

2. Use Natural and Authentic Gestures: Let your gestures flow naturally from your speech and emotions, rather than forcing or overexaggerating them. Use open, expansive gestures to emphasize key points, illustrate concepts, or convey enthusiasm. Keep your gestures in sync with your speech and avoid distracting or repetitive movements that may detract from your message.

3. Maintain Eye Contact: Establish and maintain eye contact with your audience to build rapport, convey confidence, and foster a connection. Make eye contact with individuals across the room to engage them directly and make them feel included in your presentation. Use facial expressions to convey warmth, sincerity, and empathy, and to reinforce your verbal message.

4. Match Facial Expressions to Tone and Content: Use facial expressions to reflect the tone and content of your speech, conveying emotions such as excitement, concern, surprise, or empathy. Smile warmly to convey friendliness and positivity, furrow your brow to show concern or seriousness, and widen your eyes to express surprise or enthusiasm. Your facial expressions should complement your verbal message and enhance its impact.

5. Practice Subtlety and Variation: Practice using a range of gestures and facial expressions to add nuance and depth to your communication. Experiment with subtle variations in hand movements, facial expressions, and body language to convey different emotions and meanings. Avoid repetitive or exaggerated gestures, and strive for authenticity and naturalness in your non-verbal communication.

6. Use Gestures to Reinforce Verbal Messages: Use gestures strategically to reinforce your verbal messages and make them more memorable. For example, use descriptive gestures to illustrate size, shape, or direction, or use illustrative gestures to mimic actions or movements described in your speech. Gestures can help clarify complex concepts, enhance understanding, and make your message more vivid and compelling.

7. Be Mindful of Timing and Pacing: Pay attention to the timing and pacing of your gestures and facial expressions to ensure they align with your speech and enhance its rhythm and flow. Use pauses strategically to allow your audience to absorb your message and to punctuate key points with meaningful gestures or expressions. Avoid rushing or overloading your presentation with excessive gestures, and maintain a balance between verbal and non-verbal communication.

8. Seek Feedback and Refinement: Solicit feedback from peers, mentors, or trusted advisors to evaluate your use of gestures and facial expressions during public speaking. Ask for specific feedback on your body language, facial expressions, and gestures, and use this feedback to refine and improve your non-verbal communication skills over time. Practice in front of a mirror or record yourself to observe your gestures and facial expressions objectively, and make adjustments as needed to enhance your effectiveness as a speaker.

Eye Contact and its Impact on Connection

Eye contact is a fundamental aspect of non-verbal communication that plays a crucial role in establishing a connection with your audience during public speaking. Here's how eye contact impacts connection and how to use it effectively:

1. Establishes Rapport: Eye contact helps establish a sense of rapport and connection between you and your audience. When you make eye contact with individuals in the audience, it creates a feeling of direct engagement and involvement, making them feel valued and included in your presentation. Establishing rapport through eye contact fosters a sense of trust and receptivity, making your audience more attentive and receptive to your message.

2. Enhances Engagement: Eye contact enhances audience engagement by capturing their attention and maintaining their focus throughout your speech. When you make eye contact with individuals, it encourages them to actively participate in the conversation, rather than passively listening. Engaging eye contact signals to your audience that you are genuinely interested in connecting with them and that you value their presence and participation.

3. Conveys Confidence and Authority: Confident and assertive speakers maintain consistent eye contact with their audience, conveying confidence and authority in their message. When you make eye contact with confidence, it signals to your audience that you are knowledgeable, trustworthy, and in control of the situation. Confident eye contact enhances your credibility as a speaker and instills confidence in your audience that you are someone worth listening to.

4. Builds Connection: Eye contact builds a sense of connection and intimacy between you and your audience, creating a shared experience that transcends the physical distance between you. When you make eye contact with individuals, it establishes a personal connection that goes beyond mere words, allowing you to communicate on a deeper level. Eye contact humanizes your presentation, making it more relatable and emotionally resonant for your audience.

5. Promotes Active Listening: Eye contact encourages active listening by signaling to your audience that you are attentive and receptive to their feedback. When you make eye contact with individuals, it encourages them to actively listen and engage with your message, rather than tuning out or becoming distracted. Active listening fosters a dynamic exchange of ideas between you and your audience, leading to a more meaningful and impactful communication experience.

6. Demonstrates Respect and Empathy: Making eye contact with your audience demonstrates respect and empathy for their presence and participation. It shows that you value their attention and are genuinely interested in connecting with them on a personal level. Eye contact conveys empathy by allowing you to gauge the reactions and emotions of your audience, enabling you to adjust your delivery accordingly and ensure that your message resonates with them.

7. Creates a Memorable Experience: Eye contact creates a memorable and impactful speaking experience for your audience by forging a strong emotional connection that lingers long after your presentation is over. When you make meaningful eye contact with individuals, it leaves a lasting impression and makes them feel seen, heard, and understood. A memorable speaking experience fosters a positive perception of you as a speaker and increases the likelihood that your message will be remembered and acted upon.

Utilizing Posture and Movement in Public Speaking

Utilizing posture and movement effectively is crucial for conveying confidence, engaging your audience, and enhancing the impact of your message during public speaking. Here's how to use posture and movement to your advantage:

1. Stand Tall and Confident: Adopting a strong and confident posture is essential for projecting authority and presence as a speaker. Stand tall with your shoulders back, chest open, and feet shoulder-width apart. Avoid slouching or hunching over, as this can convey insecurity or lack of confidence. A confident posture communicates to your audience that you are self-assured and capable, commanding their attention and respect.

2. Use Open and Inviting Body Language: Open and inviting body language helps create a positive and welcoming atmosphere for your audience. Keep your arms relaxed and uncrossed at your sides or use natural gestures to emphasize key points. Avoid crossing your arms or creating barriers between yourself and your audience, as this can signal defensiveness or detachment. Open body language signals to your audience that you are approachable and receptive to their feedback.

3. Move Purposefully and Intentionally: Movement can be a powerful tool for engaging your audience and emphasizing key points in your speech. Move around the stage or speaking area purposefully, using deliberate gestures and movements to reinforce your message. Avoid pacing or wandering aimlessly, as this can be distracting or disorienting for your audience. Instead, move with intention and purpose, using your body language to enhance the impact of your words.

4. Make Strategic Use of Stage Space: Utilize the entire stage space to your advantage, moving around to different areas to maintain visual interest and engagement. Use movement to transition between different points or sections of your speech, signaling to your audience that you are moving on to a new topic or idea. Vary your position on stage to keep your audience visually engaged and to create a dynamic and energetic presentation.

5. Establish Proximity and Connection: Use movement to establish proximity and connection with your audience, particularly when addressing specific individuals or groups. Move closer to your audience when delivering important points or when seeking to establish a more intimate connection. Make eye contact and use gestures to engage directly with individuals, making them feel seen and included in your presentation.

6. Match Movement to Message: Align your movements with the content and tone of your speech, using body language to reinforce your verbal message. For example, use expansive gestures to emphasize big ideas or use subtle movements to convey intimacy or vulnerability. Match your movement to the emotions and themes of your speech, creating a cohesive and impactful presentation.

7. Practice and Refine: Rehearse your posture and movement along with your speech to ensure that they enhance rather than detract from your message. Pay attention to your body language in rehearsals, making adjustments as needed to improve your posture, gestures, and movement. Seek feedback from peers or mentors to identify areas for improvement and refine your non-verbal communication skills over time.

8. Stay Authentic and Genuine: Above all, remain authentic and genuine in your use of posture and movement. Let your body language reflect your personality and style as a speaker, rather than trying to adopt a posture or movement that feels unnatural or forced. Authenticity builds trust and credibility with your audience, allowing them to connect with you on a deeper level and making your message more impactful and memorable.

Dressing for Success in Public Speaking

Dressing for success in public speaking is an important aspect of non-verbal communication that can enhance your credibility, professionalism, and overall impact as a speaker. Here are some tips for dressing appropriately for public speaking:

1. **Know Your Audience and Venue:** Consider the expectations and norms of your audience and venue when selecting your attire. Tailor your clothing choices to match the formality and context of the event, taking into account factors such as the audience demographics, venue setting, and purpose of your presentation. Dressing appropriately shows respect for your audience and demonstrates your professionalism as a speaker.

2. **Choose Appropriate Attire:** Select clothing that is appropriate for the occasion and reflects your personal style while also considering the expectations of your audience. For formal events or professional settings, opt for business attire such as a suit, dress shirt, and tie for men, or a tailored dress or pantsuit for women. For more casual or creative environments, you may have more flexibility to dress in smart casual attire, such as dress pants or a skirt paired with a blouse or collared shirt.

3. **Ensure Comfort and Confidence:** Choose clothing that makes you feel comfortable and confident, allowing you to focus on delivering your speech without distractions or discomfort. Avoid clothing that is too tight, restrictive, or uncomfortable, as this can detract from your ability to connect with your audience and deliver your message effectively. Opt for fabrics that are breathable, wrinkle-resistant, and move with your body to ensure maximum comfort and ease of movement.

4. **Pay Attention to Grooming and Hygiene:** Personal grooming and hygiene are important considerations when dressing for public speaking. Ensure that your clothing is clean, well-maintained, and free of wrinkles or stains. Pay attention to details such as grooming your hair, trimming your nails, and maintaining good oral hygiene to present a polished and professional appearance. A well-groomed appearance enhances your credibility and confidence as a speaker, helping you make a positive impression on your audience.

5. **Minimize Distractions:** Avoid clothing or accessories that may be distracting or detract from your message. Choose simple, classic styles and neutral colors that are unlikely to overshadow or clash with your presentation. Avoid excessive jewelry, loud patterns, or flashy

accessories that may draw attention away from your face or message.
The focus should be on you and your message, rather than your attire
or accessories.

6. **Consider Cultural Sensitivities:** Be mindful of cultural sensitivities
and norms when selecting your attire, especially if you are speaking to
an audience from diverse cultural backgrounds. Avoid clothing or
symbols that may be offensive or inappropriate in certain cultures, and
strive to dress in a way that is respectful and inclusive of your
audience's cultural values and customs.

7. **Prepare in Advance:** Plan your outfit in advance and ensure that it
is clean, pressed, and ready to wear on the day of your presentation.
Avoid last-minute wardrobe changes or scrambling to find suitable
attire, as this can add unnecessary stress and anxiety on the day of
your speech. By preparing your outfit in advance, you can focus your
energy and attention on delivering a confident and compelling
presentation.

8. **Project Professionalism and Confidence:** Your attire should project
professionalism, confidence, and authority as a speaker. Dressing
appropriately shows that you take your role as a speaker seriously and
are committed to delivering a high-quality presentation. Projecting
confidence and professionalism through your attire helps establish
credibility and trust with your audience, making them more receptive
to your message and more likely to engage with your presentation.

Chapter 4
The Art of Vocal Delivery

Perfecting Voice Projection and Clarity

Perfecting voice projection and clarity is essential for effective public speaking, as it ensures that your message is heard and understood by your audience. Here are some tips to help you improve your voice projection and clarity:

1. **Practice Proper Breathing Techniques:** Effective voice projection starts with proper breathing techniques. Practice diaphragmatic breathing to support your voice and project it more effectively. Inhale deeply through your nose, allowing your diaphragm to expand and your abdomen to rise, then exhale slowly through your mouth, engaging your abdominal muscles to control the flow of air. This helps you produce a strong, resonant voice that carries well in a room.

2. **Warm Up Your Voice:** Before speaking in public, warm up your voice to ensure optimal vocal clarity and projection. Perform vocal warm-up exercises such as humming, lip trills, tongue twisters, and vocal sirens to relax your vocal cords, improve resonance, and increase vocal flexibility. Warm-up exercises help prevent vocal strain and ensure that your voice sounds clear and vibrant when you speak.

3. **Maintain Proper Posture:** Good posture is essential for optimal voice projection and clarity. Stand tall with your shoulders back, chest open, and head held high to allow for unrestricted airflow and vocal resonance. Avoid slouching or collapsing your chest, as this can restrict your ability to breathe deeply and project your voice effectively. By maintaining proper posture, you create more space for your lungs to expand and produce a stronger, more resonant voice.

4. **Speak from Your Diaphragm:** Focus on speaking from your diaphragm rather than your throat or chest. Imagine that your voice is originating from your abdomen, and engage your abdominal muscles to support and project your voice. This helps you produce a fuller, more powerful sound that carries well in a room, rather than a weak or strained voice that gets lost in the background noise.

5. **Articulate Clearly:** Pay attention to your articulation and pronunciation to ensure that your words are clear and easy to

understand. Enunciate each word carefully, emphasizing consonants and vowels to ensure clarity of speech. Avoid mumbling or speaking too quickly, as this can make it difficult for your audience to follow along. Practice speaking slowly and clearly, allowing each word to be heard and understood.

6. **Modulate Your Voice:** Use vocal variety to maintain audience engagement and enhance the impact of your message. Vary your pitch, volume, pace, and tone to add interest and emphasis to your speech. Use pauses strategically to allow your audience to absorb key points and to emphasize important ideas. By modulating your voice effectively, you create a dynamic and engaging presentation that captures your audience's attention and holds their interest.

7. **Project Your Voice:** Projecting your voice involves using the appropriate volume and projection to ensure that your message reaches all members of your audience, even those seated at the back of the room. Practice speaking at a volume that is loud enough to be heard clearly by everyone in the room without straining or shouting. Imagine that you are speaking to someone at the back of the room and aim to project your voice to reach them.

8. **Use Microphone Techniques:** If using a microphone, familiarize yourself with microphone techniques to ensure optimal voice projection and clarity. Position the microphone at the appropriate distance from your mouth, typically around 6-12 inches away, and speak directly into the microphone to ensure that your voice is picked up clearly. Adjust the microphone volume as needed to avoid feedback or distortion, and speak clearly and confidently into the microphone for optimal sound quality.

Modulating Tone and Pitch for Emphasis

Modulating tone and pitch for emphasis is a powerful technique in public speaking that can enhance the impact of your message, engage your audience, and convey emotion and meaning effectively. Here are some tips to help you master this aspect of vocal delivery:

1. **Understand the Role of Tone and Pitch:** Tone refers to the quality or timbre of your voice, while pitch refers to the highness or lowness of your voice. Modulating tone and pitch involves varying these elements to convey different emotions, attitudes, and meanings in your speech. By adjusting your tone and pitch strategically, you can add emphasis, expressiveness, and nuance to your message, making it more engaging and compelling for your audience.

2. **Identify Key Points for Emphasis:** Before delivering your speech, identify the key points or ideas that you want to emphasize to your audience. These may be important concepts, key takeaways, or memorable phrases that you want to highlight for emphasis. By pinpointing these key points in advance, you can plan how to modulate your tone and pitch to draw attention to them and make them stand out in your speech.

3. **Use Inflection to Convey Meaning:** Inflection refers to the upward or downward movement of pitch in your voice as you speak. Use upward inflection to indicate questions, uncertainty, or incomplete thoughts, and downward inflection to signal statements, conclusions, or authoritative statements. By varying your inflection appropriately, you can clarify the meaning of your words and guide your audience's interpretation of your message.

4. **Experiment with Vocal Range:** Explore the full range of your vocal capabilities by experimenting with different pitches, from high to low, and tones, from soft to loud. Use higher pitches to convey excitement, enthusiasm, or urgency, and lower pitches to convey seriousness, solemnity, or intensity. Varying your vocal range adds dimension and richness to your speech, keeping your audience engaged and attentive.

5. **Match Tone and Pitch to Content:** Tailor your tone and pitch to match the content and emotional tone of your speech. Use a warm, friendly tone for storytelling or anecdotes, a passionate tone for persuasive or motivational speeches, and a calm, reassuring tone for informative or instructional presentations. Match your tone and pitch to the mood and message of your speech to create a cohesive and compelling presentation.

6. **Emphasize Keywords and Phrases:** Highlight keywords and phrases by modulating your tone and pitch to draw attention to them. Use a slightly higher pitch or increased volume to emphasize important words or phrases, and pause briefly before and after to allow them to sink in. By emphasizing key words and phrases, you signal to your audience that these are the most important points in your speech, helping to reinforce your message and increase retention.

7. **Practice Vocal Exercises:** Practice vocal exercises to improve your ability to modulate tone and pitch effectively. Exercises such as vocal scales, lip trills, and sirens can help you develop greater control and flexibility over your voice, allowing you to modulate tone and pitch more smoothly and naturally. Incorporate vocal exercises into your daily practice routine to strengthen your vocal delivery skills and enhance your overall speaking performance.

8. **Seek Feedback and Refinement:** Solicit feedback from peers, mentors, or trusted advisors to evaluate your use of tone and pitch in your public speaking. Ask for specific feedback on your ability to modulate tone and pitch effectively to convey emphasis and meaning. Use this feedback to identify areas for improvement and refine your vocal delivery skills over time. Practice regularly and continue to experiment with tone and pitch to find the right balance that resonates with your audience and enhances the impact of your message.

The Role of Pace and Pauses in Speech

The role of pace and pauses in speech is fundamental to effective public speaking. Mastering these elements can greatly enhance your ability to communicate your message clearly, engage your audience, and emphasize key points. Here's how pace and pauses influence speech:

1. **Establishing Rhythm and Flow:** Pace refers to the speed at which you deliver your speech. Maintaining a balanced pace helps establish a natural rhythm and flow to your speech, keeping your audience engaged and attentive. Speak too quickly, and your audience may struggle to keep up, leading to confusion or disinterest. Speak too

slowly, and your audience may become bored or lose focus. Finding the right pace for your speech ensures that your message is delivered clearly and effectively.

2. **Allowing Time for Absorption:** Pauses play a crucial role in speech by allowing time for your audience to absorb and process the information you're presenting. Strategic pauses give your audience a moment to reflect on what you've said, allowing them to fully digest key points or concepts. Pausing before or after important statements or transitions can help reinforce their significance and increase their impact. Pauses also create anticipation and build suspense, keeping your audience engaged and curious about what comes next.

3. **Emphasizing Key Points:** Pauses can be used strategically to emphasize key points or ideas in your speech. By pausing before or after important statements, you draw attention to them and signal to your audience that these are the most significant parts of your message. Pauses also provide a moment of emphasis, allowing your audience to fully absorb the importance of what you've said. Use pauses sparingly and purposefully to ensure maximum impact and effectiveness.

4. **Enhancing Clarity and Understanding:** Pace and pauses can enhance clarity and understanding in your speech by allowing time for your audience to process complex or unfamiliar information. Speaking too quickly can overwhelm your audience and make it difficult for them to follow along, while speaking too slowly can lead to boredom or confusion. By pacing your speech appropriately and incorporating strategic pauses, you give your audience time to grasp the content and connect with your message more effectively.

5. **Building Tension and Drama:** Pauses can also be used to build tension and drama in your speech, adding interest and excitement to your delivery. Strategic pauses before revealing important information or during dramatic moments create anticipation and suspense, keeping your audience on the edge of their seats. Pauses can heighten the emotional impact of your speech, allowing you to connect with your audience on a deeper level and evoke a stronger response.

6. **Adjusting Pace for Emphasis:** Varying your pace throughout your speech can add interest and emphasis to your delivery. Speed up during energetic or exciting parts of your speech to convey enthusiasm and passion, and slow down during more reflective or serious moments to convey depth and significance. Adjusting your pace in this way helps maintain audience engagement and highlights the emotional and thematic shifts in your message.

7. **Creating a Memorable Delivery:** Mastering pace and pauses contributes to a memorable delivery that leaves a lasting impression on your audience. A well-paced speech with strategic pauses is easier to follow and more engaging for listeners, increasing the likelihood that they will remember and act upon your message. By effectively controlling your pace and incorporating purposeful pauses, you can deliver a speech that captivates your audience and resonates with them long after it's over.

Articulating Words and Pronunciation

Articulating words and pronunciation effectively is crucial for clear and understandable communication during public speaking. Here are some tips to help you improve your articulation and pronunciation:

1. **Enunciate Clearly:** Focus on pronouncing each word clearly and distinctly to ensure that your audience can understand you. Pay attention to consonants and vowels, articulating them fully to avoid slurring or mumbling. Practice enunciating difficult words or sounds to improve clarity and precision in your speech.

2. **Slow Down Your Speech:** Speaking too quickly can lead to unclear articulation and poor pronunciation. Slow down your speech to give yourself time to pronounce each word properly and allow your audience to follow along more easily. Take a breath between phrases to pace yourself and maintain clarity throughout your presentation.

3. **Practice Tongue Twisters:** Tongue twisters are a fun and effective way to improve your articulation and pronunciation skills. Practice tongue twisters regularly to strengthen your tongue, lips, and vocal

muscles, making it easier to articulate words clearly and fluently. Start with simple tongue twisters and gradually work your way up to more challenging ones as your skills improve.

4. **Focus on Problem Sounds:** Identify any sounds or phonemes that you struggle to pronounce correctly and focus on practicing them individually. Use resources such as pronunciation guides, online tutorials, or speech therapy exercises to target problem sounds and improve your pronunciation. Practice these sounds in isolation and in the context of words, sentences, and phrases to ensure mastery.

5. **Use Mouth Exercises:** Incorporate mouth exercises into your warm-up routine to improve articulation and pronunciation. Simple exercises such as lip trills, tongue twirls, and jaw stretches can help loosen up your facial muscles and improve control over your articulators. Practice these exercises regularly to increase flexibility and agility in your mouth and improve your ability to articulate words clearly.

6. **Record Yourself:** Record yourself speaking and listen back to evaluate your articulation and pronunciation. Pay attention to any areas where your speech is unclear or difficult to understand, and make note of specific sounds or words that need improvement. By identifying areas for improvement, you can target them more effectively in your practice sessions and gradually improve your overall articulation and pronunciation skills.

7. **Seek Feedback:** Solicit feedback from peers, mentors, or speech professionals to assess your articulation and pronunciation. Ask for specific feedback on clarity, diction, and pronunciation, and use this feedback to identify areas for improvement. Consider working with a speech coach or taking a pronunciation class to receive personalized instruction and guidance on improving your articulation and pronunciation skills.

8. **Practice Regularly:** Like any skill, articulating words and pronunciation require regular practice and repetition to master. Incorporate articulation and pronunciation exercises into your daily practice routine to build muscle memory and improve your clarity and precision over time. Consistent practice will help you develop stronger

articulation and pronunciation skills and become a more confident and effective communicator.

Using Vocal Variety to Maintain Interest

Using vocal variety is a powerful technique in public speaking that can help maintain audience interest, emphasize key points, and convey emotion and meaning effectively. Here are some strategies to help you utilize vocal variety in your speeches:

1. **Vary Your Pitch:** Experiment with different pitches in your voice to add interest and emphasis to your speech. Use higher pitches to convey excitement, enthusiasm, or urgency, and lower pitches to convey seriousness, solemnity, or intensity. Varying your pitch throughout your speech helps maintain audience engagement and adds depth and richness to your delivery.

2. **Adjust Your Volume:** Modulate your volume to draw attention to important points or to create a sense of drama or intensity. Speak louder to emphasize key points or to command attention, and speak softer to create a sense of intimacy or to encourage reflection. Adjusting your volume effectively helps keep your audience engaged and adds dynamic contrast to your speech.

3. **Control Your Pace:** Vary your pace throughout your speech to keep your audience engaged and to emphasize key points. Speed up during energetic or exciting parts of your speech to convey enthusiasm and passion, and slow down during more reflective or serious moments to convey depth and significance. Adjusting your pace helps maintain audience interest and adds texture and rhythm to your delivery.

4. **Use Pauses Strategically:** Incorporate strategic pauses into your speech to add emphasis, create anticipation, and allow time for reflection. Pause briefly before or after important points to draw attention to them and to give your audience a moment to absorb the information. Pausing can also create suspense and build tension, keeping your audience engaged and curious about what comes next.

5. **Experiment with Tone:** Explore different tones in your voice to convey different emotions, attitudes, and meanings in your speech. Use a warm, friendly tone for storytelling or anecdotes, a passionate tone for persuasive or motivational speeches, and a calm, reassuring tone for informative or instructional presentations. Varying your tone adds nuance and depth to your delivery and helps you connect with your audience on an emotional level.

6. **Express Emotion and Enthusiasm:** Infuse your speech with genuine emotion and enthusiasm to captivate your audience and keep them engaged. Let your passion and conviction shine through in your voice, and use vocal cues such as intonation, rhythm, and volume to convey emotion and energy. Expressing emotion and enthusiasm helps create a connection with your audience and makes your message more compelling and memorable.

7. **Highlight Keywords and Phrases:** Use vocal variety to emphasize keywords and phrases in your speech, drawing attention to them and signaling their importance. Use changes in pitch, volume, or tone to highlight key words or phrases, and pause briefly before or after to allow them to sink in. Emphasizing keywords and phrases helps reinforce your message and increases its impact and effectiveness.

8. **Practice Vocal Exercises:** Incorporate vocal exercises into your practice routine to improve your ability to use vocal variety effectively. Practice exercises such as vocal scales, lip trills, and tongue twisters to increase flexibility and control in your voice and to develop greater range and expression. Regular vocal exercises help strengthen your vocal muscles and improve your overall vocal delivery.

Chapter 5
Connecting with Your Audience

Building Rapport and Establishing Trust

Building rapport and establishing trust with your audience are essential components of effective public speaking. When you connect with your audience on a personal level, you create a supportive and engaging environment that enhances communication and fosters a positive experience for both you and your listeners. Here are some strategies to help you build rapport and establish trust with your audience:

1. **Show Authenticity:** Be genuine and authentic in your interactions with your audience. Share personal stories, anecdotes, or experiences that demonstrate your humanity and vulnerability. Authenticity builds trust and credibility with your audience, making them more receptive to your message and more likely to connect with you on a deeper level.

2. **Demonstrate Empathy:** Show empathy and understanding towards your audience by acknowledging their needs, concerns, and perspectives. Take the time to listen to their questions, comments, and feedback, and respond with empathy and compassion. Demonstrating empathy creates a sense of connection and mutual respect, fostering a supportive and inclusive environment where everyone feels valued and heard.

3. **Use Relatable Language:** Use language that is clear, concise, and relatable to your audience. Avoid jargon, technical terms, or complex language that may alienate or confuse your listeners. Instead, use everyday language that resonates with your audience and speaks to their experiences, interests, and concerns. Using relatable language helps bridge the gap between you and your audience, making your message more accessible and engaging.

4. **Establish Common Ground:** Find common ground with your audience by identifying shared values, interests, or experiences. Highlighting commonalities helps create a sense of unity and connection, building rapport and trust between you and your audience. Look for opportunities to connect with your audience on a personal level and to create a sense of camaraderie and belonging.

5. **Maintain Eye Contact:** Make eye contact with your audience to establish rapport and create a sense of connection. Direct eye contact communicates confidence, sincerity, and engagement, making your audience feel seen and acknowledged. Scan the room and make eye contact with individuals throughout your speech to create a sense of intimacy and connection with your audience.

6. **Encourage Interaction:** Encourage interaction and engagement with your audience by inviting questions, comments, or participation throughout your speech. Create opportunities for dialogue and discussion, and be responsive and attentive to your audience's input. Encouraging interaction fosters a sense of collaboration and partnership, building rapport and trust between you and your audience.

7. **Be Transparent and Honest:** Be transparent and honest in your communication with your audience. Share relevant information, insights, or perspectives openly and honestly, even if it means admitting mistakes or vulnerabilities. Transparency builds trust and credibility with your audience, demonstrating integrity and authenticity in your communication.

8. **Follow Up and Follow Through:** Follow up with your audience after your speech to reinforce the connection and continue the conversation. Respond to questions, comments, or feedback promptly and thoughtfully, and follow through on any commitments or promises you've made. Following up demonstrates your commitment to building and maintaining a meaningful relationship with your audience, reinforcing trust and rapport over time.

Understanding Audience Psychology

Understanding audience psychology is essential for connecting with your audience effectively and delivering a compelling presentation. By gaining insight into the mindset, preferences, and behaviors of your audience, you can tailor your message and delivery to resonate with them more deeply. Here are some key aspects of audience psychology to consider:

1. **Identify Audience Needs and Interests:** Before delivering your speech, take the time to research and understand the needs, interests, and expectations of your audience. Consider their demographics, such as age, gender, occupation, and cultural background, as well as their interests, preferences, and concerns related to the topic of your presentation. By understanding what matters most to your audience, you can tailor your message to address their specific needs and interests, making it more relevant and engaging for them.

2. **Create Emotional Connection:** Emotions play a powerful role in shaping audience responses and perceptions. Tap into your audience's emotions by telling stories, sharing personal experiences, or using vivid language and imagery that evoke feelings of empathy, inspiration, or excitement. Creating an emotional connection with your audience helps them connect with your message on a deeper level and makes it more memorable and impactful.

3. **Appeal to Core Values and Beliefs:** People are more likely to respond positively to messages that align with their core values, beliefs, and identity. Identify common values and beliefs shared by your audience, such as integrity, honesty, community, or innovation, and frame your message in a way that resonates with these values. By appealing to your audience's core values and beliefs, you can build trust and rapport and increase the likelihood that they will be receptive to your message.

4. **Address Audience Concerns and Objections:** Anticipate and address potential concerns or objections that your audience may have about your message or topic. Acknowledge any skepticism, doubts, or opposing viewpoints, and provide evidence, examples, or explanations to address them effectively. By demonstrating empathy and understanding for your audience's perspective, you can build credibility and trust and increase the likelihood that they will be open to considering your message.

5. **Use Social Proof and Authority:** People are influenced by the opinions and actions of others, particularly those they perceive as credible or authoritative. Use social proof by sharing testimonials, case studies, or success stories that demonstrate the positive impact of your

message or ideas. Additionally, leverage your own expertise, credentials, or experience to establish yourself as a trusted authority on the topic. By leveraging social proof and authority, you can build credibility and trust with your audience and increase their confidence in your message.

6. **Facilitate Engagement and Interaction:** Engage your audience actively throughout your presentation by encouraging interaction, participation, and feedback. Use interactive techniques such as asking questions, conducting polls or surveys, or facilitating small group discussions to involve your audience in the learning process. By involving your audience directly, you create a sense of ownership and investment in the presentation, increasing their engagement and receptivity to your message.

7. **Adapt to Audience Dynamics:** Pay attention to audience dynamics and adapt your presentation style and delivery accordingly. Monitor audience reactions, body language, and feedback cues to gauge their level of engagement and understanding. Adjust your pace, tone, or content as needed to maintain audience interest and address any challenges or concerns that arise. By remaining flexible and responsive to audience dynamics, you can ensure that your message resonates effectively with your audience.

8. **Seek Feedback and Evaluation:** After your presentation, seek feedback and evaluation from your audience to gain insights into their perceptions, preferences, and areas for improvement. Encourage honest feedback and constructive criticism, and use it to refine your presentation skills and adapt your approach for future presentations. By actively seeking feedback and evaluation, you demonstrate your commitment to continuous improvement and to meeting the needs and expectations of your audience.

Adapting Your Message to Different Audiences

Adapting your message to different audiences is a crucial skill in public speaking that allows you to connect with diverse groups of people and effectively communicate your message to each specific audience. Here are some strategies to help you tailor your message to different audiences:

1. **Research Your Audience:** Before delivering your speech, take the time to research and understand your audience's demographics, interests, values, and preferences. Consider factors such as age, gender, occupation, education level, cultural background, and prior knowledge of the topic. Use this information to customize your message and delivery to resonate with the specific needs and interests of your audience.

2. **Identify Common Ground:** Find common ground with your audience by identifying shared values, experiences, or interests. Highlighting commonalities helps create a sense of connection and rapport with your audience, making it easier to engage and persuade them. Look for opportunities to relate your message to their experiences or concerns, and frame it in a way that speaks to their interests and aspirations.

3. **Tailor Your Content:** Adapt your content to match the interests, knowledge level, and preferences of your audience. Customize your examples, anecdotes, and illustrations to be relevant and relatable to your audience's experiences and interests. Use language and terminology that is familiar and accessible to your audience, avoiding jargon or technical terms that may be confusing or alienating.

4. **Adjust Your Tone and Style:** Adapt your tone and style of delivery to match the preferences and expectations of your audience. Consider the formality of the occasion, as well as the cultural norms and communication styles of your audience. For example, if speaking to a formal or conservative audience, adopt a more formal tone and delivery style. If speaking to a casual or informal audience, you may use a more conversational tone and delivery style.

5. **Address Specific Concerns:** Anticipate and address specific concerns or objections that your audience may have about your message. Tailor your content to address their questions, doubts, or objections, and provide evidence, examples, or explanations to alleviate their concerns. By demonstrating empathy and understanding for your

audience's perspective, you can build trust and credibility and increase the likelihood that they will be receptive to your message.

6. **Consider Cultural Sensitivities:** Be mindful of cultural differences and sensitivities when adapting your message to different audiences. Respect cultural norms, values, and customs, and avoid language or topics that may be offensive or inappropriate in certain cultural contexts. Tailor your message to be inclusive and respectful of diverse cultural backgrounds, ensuring that all members of your audience feel valued and included.

7. **Customize Your Delivery:** Customize your delivery to match the preferences and expectations of your audience. Pay attention to factors such as vocal tone, body language, and presentation style, and adjust them accordingly to connect with your audience more effectively. For example, if speaking to a younger audience, you may use more dynamic and interactive presentation techniques. If speaking to an older audience, you may use a more formal and authoritative presentation style.

8. **Seek Feedback and Adaptation:** After delivering your speech, seek feedback from your audience to evaluate the effectiveness of your message and delivery. Pay attention to their reactions, comments, and questions, and use them to identify areas for improvement and adaptation. Continuously seek feedback and make adjustments to your message and delivery based on the needs and preferences of each specific audience.

Handling Questions and Interactions

Handling questions and interactions effectively is an essential aspect of connecting with your audience during public speaking. Here are some strategies to help you manage questions and interactions confidently:

1. **Encourage Interaction:** Encourage audience interaction throughout your presentation by inviting questions, comments, and feedback. Let your audience know that their participation is welcome and valued, and create opportunities for them to engage with you and each other.

Encouraging interaction fosters a sense of collaboration and partnership, making your presentation more engaging and interactive.

2. **Set Expectations:** Set clear expectations for how and when you will handle questions and interactions during your presentation. Let your audience know whether you prefer questions to be asked during the presentation or saved for a designated Q&A session at the end. Establishing clear guidelines helps manage audience expectations and ensures a smooth and organized interaction process.

3. **Listen Actively:** Listen attentively to questions and comments from your audience, and demonstrate active listening by making eye contact, nodding, and acknowledging their input. Show genuine interest and curiosity in their questions, and avoid interrupting or dismissing their contributions. Actively listening to your audience builds rapport and trust and fosters a positive and respectful interaction environment.

4. **Repeat and Clarify:** Repeat or paraphrase questions before answering them to ensure that everyone in the audience hears and understands the question. Clarify any ambiguous or unclear aspects of the question to ensure that you address the audience member's intended meaning. Rephrasing questions also gives you time to process and formulate your response effectively.

5. **Stay Calm and Confident:** Maintain a calm and confident demeanor when handling questions and interactions, even if you're unsure of the answer or faced with challenging questions. Take a deep breath and compose yourself before responding, and speak clearly and confidently to convey authority and expertise. Remember that it's okay to admit when you don't know the answer, and offer to follow up with additional information later if needed.

6. **Be Respectful and Inclusive:** Treat all audience members with respect and courtesy, regardless of their questions or comments. Avoid making judgments or assumptions based on the content or tone of their questions, and respond in a respectful and inclusive manner. Create a safe and supportive environment where all voices are heard and

valued, and where everyone feels comfortable participating in the discussion.

7. **Keep Responses Concise and Relevant:** Keep your responses concise and relevant to the question being asked, and avoid going off on tangents or delving into unrelated topics. Focus on addressing the audience member's question directly and providing a clear and informative response. If necessary, offer to discuss related topics further after the presentation or during a follow-up conversation.

8. **Manage Time Effectively:** Manage your time effectively when handling questions and interactions to ensure that you cover all relevant topics and maintain the overall flow of your presentation. Set limits on the length of responses and the number of questions to be addressed, and be prepared to gracefully move on if time constraints become an issue. Prioritize questions that are most relevant and beneficial to the majority of the audience, and offer to follow up with individual audience members as needed.

Using Humor Appropriately in Public Speaking

Using humor appropriately in public speaking can be a powerful tool for connecting with your audience, lightening the mood, and enhancing engagement. However, it's essential to use humor thoughtfully and tactfully to ensure that it aligns with your message and resonates positively with your audience. Here are some tips for using humor effectively in public speaking:

1. **Know Your Audience:** Before incorporating humor into your speech, take the time to understand your audience's demographics, interests, and cultural background. Tailor your humor to match the preferences and sensibilities of your audience, avoiding jokes or references that may be offensive or inappropriate. Consider the age, gender, ethnicity, and professional background of your audience when selecting humor that will resonate with them.

2. **Keep it Relevant:** Use humor that is relevant to your topic and message to ensure that it enhances rather than detracts from your

presentation. Integrate humor seamlessly into your speech by tying it to key points, anecdotes, or examples that illustrate your message. Avoid using humor solely for the sake of entertainment, as it may come across as superficial or disconnected from the content of your speech.

3. **Use Self-Deprecating Humor:** Self-deprecating humor, where you poke fun at yourself or your own experiences, can be particularly effective in public speaking. It helps to humanize you as a speaker, making you more relatable and approachable to your audience. However, be mindful of striking the right balance between self-deprecation and self-confidence, ensuring that your humor does not undermine your credibility or authority as a speaker.

4. **Be Positive and Inclusive:** Use humor that is positive and inclusive, avoiding jokes that rely on stereotypes, discrimination, or divisive topics. Aim to uplift and inspire your audience with your humor, creating a sense of camaraderie and connection. Be mindful of the impact your humor may have on different members of your audience, and strive to create an inclusive and welcoming environment for all.

5. **Keep it Clean:** Avoid using humor that is offensive, vulgar, or inappropriate for a professional setting. Keep your humor clean and family-friendly, ensuring that it is suitable for all members of your audience, including children and sensitive listeners. Err on the side of caution when selecting jokes or humorous anecdotes, and avoid topics that may be controversial or potentially offensive to some audience members.

6. **Practice Timing and Delivery:** Pay attention to timing and delivery when using humor in your speech. Practice delivering your jokes with good timing, pacing, and emphasis to maximize their impact and effectiveness. Use pauses and facial expressions to cue your audience to laugh, and be prepared to adjust your delivery based on their response. Practice your humor repeatedly to ensure that it flows naturally and fits seamlessly into your speech.

7. **Be Authentic:** Use humor that reflects your genuine personality and style as a speaker. Avoid forcing humor or trying to imitate someone else's comedic style, as it may come across as insincere or inauthentic.

Be yourself and let your natural sense of humor shine through, allowing your audience to connect with you on a personal level.

8. **Be Prepared for Different Reactions:** Be prepared for different reactions to your humor, including laughter, silence, or even occasional groans or polite chuckles. Not every joke will land perfectly, and that's okay. Stay confident and resilient, and continue with your presentation without dwelling on any moments that fall flat. Remember that humor is subjective, and what one person finds funny, another may not.

Chapter 6
Effective Use of Visual Aids

Selecting and Designing Visual Aids

Selecting and designing visual aids is crucial for enhancing the effectiveness of your public speaking presentations. Visual aids can help clarify complex information, reinforce key points, and engage your audience visually. Here are some tips for selecting and designing effective visual aids:

1. **Understand Your Audience:** Consider the demographics, preferences, and learning styles of your audience when selecting and designing visual aids. Choose visuals that will resonate with your audience and effectively convey your message. For example, if your audience consists of visual learners, consider using diagrams, charts, or images to illustrate key concepts.

2. **Align with Your Message:** Ensure that your visual aids align with the content and objectives of your presentation. Select visuals that support and enhance your message, rather than detract from it. Avoid using unnecessary or distracting visuals that do not contribute to the overall understanding of your presentation.

3. **Keep it Simple:** Use simple and clear visuals that are easy to understand and digest. Avoid cluttered or overly complex visuals that may confuse or overwhelm your audience. Simplify information into digestible chunks and use visuals to highlight key points or trends effectively.

4. **Use High-Quality Graphics:** Use high-quality graphics and images that are clear, crisp, and visually appealing. Avoid using low-resolution or pixelated images that may detract from the professionalism of your presentation. Invest in high-quality graphics or design software to create polished and professional-looking visual aids.

5. **Emphasize Visual Hierarchy:** Use visual hierarchy to prioritize information and guide the viewer's attention. Arrange visual elements in a logical and organized manner, with important information emphasized through size, color, or placement. Use headings, bullet points, or call-out boxes to draw attention to key points effectively.

6. **Choose Appropriate Formats:** Select visual aids that are appropriate for the content and context of your presentation. Consider using a variety of formats, such as slideshows, videos, posters, or handouts, to accommodate different learning styles and presentation settings. Choose formats that are accessible and easy to view from various distances and angles.

7. **Design for Readability:** Ensure that your visual aids are easy to read and understand from a distance. Use large, legible fonts and high-contrast colors to maximize readability, particularly in large auditoriums or conference rooms. Avoid using decorative fonts or low-contrast color combinations that may be difficult to read.

8. **Practice Consistency:** Maintain consistency in the design and formatting of your visual aids to create a cohesive and professional look. Use consistent fonts, colors, and styles throughout your presentation to reinforce your branding and make your visuals more visually appealing. Avoid mixing multiple design styles or visual elements that may create visual clutter or confusion.

9. **Keep it Relevant:** Ensure that your visual aids are relevant and directly related to the content of your presentation. Avoid using generic or stock visuals that do not add value to your message. Customize your visual aids to fit the specific context and objectives of your presentation, using relevant data, examples, or illustrations to support your points effectively.

10. **Seek Feedback:** Before finalizing your visual aids, seek feedback from colleagues, mentors, or trusted advisors. Ask for feedback on the clarity, relevance, and effectiveness of your visuals, and make any necessary revisions based on their input. Testing your visual aids with a small audience or focus group can also help identify any potential issues or areas for improvement.

Integrating Slides, Props, and Videos

Integrating slides, props, and videos effectively can significantly enhance the impact and engagement of your public speaking presentations. Here are some strategies for effectively integrating these visual aids into your speeches:

1. **Slides:**
  - Keep slides simple and uncluttered: Use concise bullet points, clear visuals, and minimal text to convey key points effectively.
  - Use consistent formatting: Maintain a consistent design theme, font style, and color scheme throughout your slides to create a cohesive and professional look.
  - Emphasize visuals over text: Use visuals such as images, charts, and diagrams to convey information whenever possible, rather than relying solely on text.
  - Limit the number of slides: Avoid overwhelming your audience with too many slides. Aim for around 1-2 slides per minute of speaking time to maintain audience engagement.
  - Use transitions and animations sparingly: While transitions and animations can add visual interest, use them sparingly to avoid distracting from your message.

2. **Props:**
  - Choose props that enhance your message: Select props that are relevant to your topic and help illustrate key points or concepts in your speech.
  - Keep props simple and unobtrusive: Avoid using props that are too large, complex, or cumbersome to handle during your presentation. Choose props that are easy to transport and set up on stage.
  - Practice with props beforehand: Familiarize yourself with how to use your props effectively during your presentation. Practice handling and incorporating props into your speech to ensure smooth execution on stage.
  - Use props strategically: Introduce props at appropriate moments in your speech to emphasize key points or add visual interest. Be mindful of the timing and placement of props to maximize their impact on your audience.

3. **Videos:**
  - Choose videos that complement your message: Select videos that support and enhance the content of your speech, rather than detracting from it. Ensure that videos are relevant, high-quality, and appropriate for your audience.

- Embed videos seamlessly into your presentation: Integrate videos into your slides or presentation software so that they play seamlessly during your speech. Test video playback beforehand to ensure smooth operation during your presentation.
- Keep videos short and engaging: Aim for videos that are no longer than a few minutes in length to maintain audience engagement. Choose videos that are visually compelling, emotionally resonant, or informative to capture your audience's attention.
- Provide context before and after the video: Introduce each video with a brief explanation of its relevance to your speech, and provide a summary or reflection afterward to tie it back to your main points.

4. Practice Integration:

- Rehearse integrating visual aids into your speech: Practice incorporating slides, props, and videos into your speech during rehearsals to ensure smooth integration on stage. Pay attention to transitions between different visual aids and adjust your timing and pacing as needed.
- Maintain eye contact and engagement: While using visual aids, continue to maintain eye contact with your audience and engage them actively throughout your speech. Use visual aids as supporting tools to reinforce your message, rather than relying on them as a crutch.

Ensuring Visual Aids Enhance, Not Distract

Ensuring that visual aids enhance rather than distract from your public speaking presentation is crucial for maintaining audience engagement and conveying your message effectively. Here are some strategies to help you ensure that your visual aids enhance your presentation:

1. Relevance to the Message:

- Ensure that your visual aids directly support and reinforce the key points of your presentation. Choose visuals that clarify complex concepts, provide additional context, or illustrate examples relevant to your message.
- Avoid using visual aids that are tangential or unrelated to your main message. Every visual should serve a purpose in enhancing audience understanding and retention of your content.

2. Simplicity and Clarity:

   - Keep your visual aids simple and easy to understand. Avoid cluttering slides with excessive text, complex diagrams, or irrelevant images.

   - Use clear and concise visuals that convey your message at a glance. Aim for simplicity in design and layout to minimize distractions and focus audience attention on the key points of your presentation.

3. Consistency in Design:

   - Maintain a consistent design theme throughout your visual aids, including slides, props, and videos. Use a cohesive color scheme, font style, and formatting to create a professional and polished look.

   - Consistency in design helps create a visual hierarchy that guides audience attention to the most important elements of your presentation.

4. Limited Use of Text:

   - Limit the amount of text on your visual aids to essential information only. Use bullet points or short phrases to convey key points, rather than lengthy paragraphs.

   - Avoid reading directly from your slides or other visual aids. Use them as prompts to guide your presentation, while providing additional explanation and context verbally.

5. Visual Variety:

   - Incorporate a variety of visual elements to maintain audience interest and engagement. Use a combination of slides, props, videos, and other visuals to illustrate different aspects of your presentation.

   - Mix up the types of visuals you use to keep the presentation dynamic and engaging. For example, use charts and graphs to present data, photos and images to illustrate concepts, and videos to provide real-life examples or demonstrations.

6. Practice and Timing:

   - Practice using your visual aids during rehearsals to ensure smooth integration into your presentation. Familiarize yourself with the timing and flow of your visual aids to avoid awkward transitions or technical glitches during the actual presentation.

- Time your presentation carefully to allow sufficient opportunity for your audience to absorb and engage with each visual aid. Avoid rushing through slides or other visuals, and give your audience time to process the information before moving on to the next point.

7. **Engage with Visual Aids:**
   - Interact with your visual aids to draw attention to key points and facilitate audience understanding. Use gestures, pointers, or annotations to highlight important information and guide audience attention.
   - Maintain eye contact with your audience while using visual aids, and gauge their reactions to ensure they are following along and engaged with your presentation.

Rehearsing with Visuals for Seamless Delivery

Rehearsing with visuals is essential for achieving a seamless and effective delivery in your public speaking presentations. Here's how you can rehearse with visuals to ensure a polished performance:

1. Familiarize Yourself with the Visuals:
   - Before you begin rehearsing with visuals, familiarize yourself with the content and layout of each visual aid. Review your slides, props, or videos to ensure that you understand how they support your message and flow together within your presentation.

2. Practice with Timing and Transitions:
   - Practice your presentation with visuals multiple times to get comfortable with the timing and transitions between each visual aid. Time your delivery to ensure that you allow enough time for each visual to be fully understood and absorbed by your audience.

3. Coordinate Visuals with Verbal Delivery:
   - Coordinate your verbal delivery with the visuals to ensure that they complement each other seamlessly. Practice speaking while advancing slides or using props to ensure that your verbal explanations align with what is being presented visually.

4. Focus on Smooth Integration:

- Pay attention to how you integrate visuals into your presentation to ensure a smooth and natural flow. Practice transitioning between speaking and showing visuals to avoid awkward pauses or technical issues during your presentation.

5. Rehearse Technical Aspects:

- If using technology for your visuals, such as slideshows or videos, rehearse the technical aspects of their presentation. Ensure that you know how to operate any equipment or software needed to display visuals, and practice troubleshooting common issues.

6. Seek Feedback and Make Adjustments:

- Rehearse your presentation with visuals in front of a trusted friend, colleague, or mentor and solicit feedback on your delivery. Pay attention to their suggestions for improvement and make any necessary adjustments to your visual aids or delivery based on their feedback.

7. Practice Non-Verbal Communication:

- Practice incorporating non-verbal communication, such as gestures and facial expressions, while using visuals to enhance your message. Use visual aids as opportunities to engage with your audience and reinforce key points through your body language.

8. Time Your Rehearsals:

- Time your rehearsals with visuals to ensure that your presentation fits within the allotted time frame. Aim to strike a balance between allowing sufficient time for each visual aid and maintaining an overall pace that keeps your audience engaged.

9. Record Yourself for Review:

- Record yourself rehearsing with visuals and review the recording to identify areas for improvement. Pay attention to your delivery, pacing, and how effectively you integrate visuals into your presentation.

10. Repeat and Refine:

- Repeat the rehearsal process multiple times, making adjustments as needed to improve your delivery with visuals. Refine your timing, transitions, and overall presentation until you feel confident and comfortable with the seamless integration of visuals.

Dealing with Technical Challenges in Presentations

Dealing with technical challenges during presentations is a common concern for public speakers. However, with proper preparation and a calm approach, you can effectively navigate and mitigate potential issues. Here's how to handle technical challenges when using visual aids during your presentation:

1. **Arrive Early and Test Equipment:**
   - Arrive at the venue well before your presentation to allow ample time for setup and testing of equipment. Test all audiovisual equipment, including projectors, screens, microphones, and any other devices you'll be using. Ensure that everything is functioning properly and that your visuals display correctly.

2. **Have Backup Plans:**
   - Prepare backup plans in case of technical failures. Bring spare batteries, cables, adapters, and any other necessary equipment. Consider storing your presentation on multiple devices (e.g., USB drive, cloud storage) in case one fails. Additionally, have printed copies of your presentation slides as a last resort.

3. **Familiarize Yourself with Equipment:**
   - Familiarize yourself with the venue's audiovisual equipment and operating procedures beforehand. If possible, practice using the equipment during a site visit or rehearsal. Knowing how to troubleshoot common issues, such as adjusting screen resolution or switching input sources, can help you quickly address problems during your presentation.

4. **Stay Calm and Confident:**
   - If technical issues arise during your presentation, remain calm and composed. Panicking or showing frustration can undermine your credibility and distract your audience. Take a deep breath, assess the situation calmly, and focus on finding a solution.

5. Engage the Audience:

   - Use technical difficulties as an opportunity to engage with your audience. Acknowledge the issue with a touch of humor or empathy to lighten the mood. Engage the audience in a brief discussion or activity while the problem is being resolved to keep them engaged and maintain momentum.

6. Seek Assistance:

   - Don't hesitate to seek assistance from event staff or technical support personnel if you encounter technical challenges that you can't resolve on your own. Event staff are typically trained to handle technical issues and can provide guidance or troubleshooting assistance.

7. Keep Presenting Without Visuals:

   - If all else fails and you're unable to resolve the technical issue promptly, consider continuing with your presentation without visuals. Use verbal explanations, storytelling, or audience engagement techniques to convey your message effectively without relying on visual aids.

8. Maintain Flexibility:

   - Be prepared to adapt your presentation on the fly if necessary. If technical issues prevent you from presenting certain visuals or slides, be flexible and ready to adjust your content accordingly. Focus on delivering your message in the most effective way possible given the circumstances.

9. Follow Up Afterward:

   - After your presentation, take the time to follow up with event organizers or technical support personnel to provide feedback on any technical issues you encountered. Constructive feedback can help improve future presentations and prevent similar challenges from occurring again.

Chapter 7
Overcoming Public Speaking Anxiety

Identifying and Understanding Fear of Public Speaking

Identifying and understanding fear of public speaking is essential for effectively overcoming this common challenge. Here are some key aspects to consider:

1. **Physical Symptoms:**
   - Pay attention to physical symptoms that may accompany fear of public speaking, such as sweating, trembling, rapid heartbeat, dry mouth, or feeling faint. These physical manifestations are common responses to the body's natural stress response when faced with a perceived threat.

2. **Cognitive Symptoms:**
   - Notice any cognitive symptoms associated with fear of public speaking, such as racing thoughts, negative self-talk, or catastrophic thinking. Fearful individuals often experience intrusive thoughts about potential failures, embarrassment, or negative judgments from the audience.

3. **Emotional Responses:**
   - Recognize the emotional responses that arise from fear of public speaking, such as anxiety, nervousness, dread, or panic. These emotions can be intense and overwhelming, making it challenging to remain calm and composed during public speaking engagements.

4. **Underlying Causes:**
   - Explore the underlying causes of your fear of public speaking. Common factors may include past negative experiences, lack of confidence or self-esteem, fear of failure or rejection, perfectionism, or social anxiety. Understanding the root causes can help you address them more effectively.

5. **Self-Awareness:**
   - Cultivate self-awareness by reflecting on your thoughts, feelings, and behaviors related to public speaking. Identify specific triggers that exacerbate your fear and notice how your body and mind respond in

these situations. Awareness of your fear patterns is the first step towards overcoming them.

6. Social Comparison:

- Avoid comparing yourself to others or holding unrealistic standards for public speaking performance. Remember that everyone experiences some degree of nervousness or anxiety when speaking in public, and it's okay to feel nervous. Focus on improving your own skills and confidence rather than trying to be perfect.

7. Perceived Threats:

- Examine the perceived threats that contribute to your fear of public speaking. These threats may include fear of judgment or criticism from the audience, fear of making mistakes or forgetting your lines, or fear of being embarrassed or humiliated in front of others. Challenge these irrational beliefs with evidence and logical reasoning.

8. Mindset Shift:

- Shift your mindset from viewing public speaking as a threat to seeing it as an opportunity for growth and self-expression. Embrace the challenge of public speaking as a chance to share your knowledge, connect with others, and make a positive impact. Reframe nervous energy as excitement and anticipation rather than fear.

9. Gradual Exposure:

- Gradually expose yourself to speaking opportunities to desensitize yourself to the fear of public speaking. Start with low-pressure situations, such as speaking to friends or family members, then gradually progress to larger audiences or more formal speaking engagements. Each successful experience will boost your confidence and reduce anxiety over time.

10. Seek Support:

- Don't hesitate to seek support from trusted friends, mentors, or professionals if you're struggling to overcome your fear of public speaking. Consider joining a public speaking group or enrolling in a public speaking course to gain practical skills and receive constructive feedback in a supportive environment.

Practical Strategies for Managing Anxiety

Managing anxiety while public speaking is crucial for delivering confident and effective presentations. Here are practical strategies to help you overcome public speaking anxiety:

1. **Preparation and Practice:**
   - Thoroughly prepare your speech or presentation content. Practice speaking aloud multiple times, focusing on clarity, pacing, and emphasis. Rehearsing your presentation can help build confidence and familiarity with your material, reducing anxiety.

2. **Visualization and Positive Imagery:**
   - Visualize yourself delivering a successful presentation. Imagine yourself speaking confidently, engaging the audience, and receiving positive feedback. Positive visualization can help alleviate anxiety and increase self-assurance.

3. **Deep Breathing and Relaxation Techniques:**
   - Practice deep breathing exercises and relaxation techniques to calm your nerves before speaking. Take slow, deep breaths to activate the body's relaxation response and reduce physiological symptoms of anxiety, such as rapid heartbeat or shallow breathing.

4. **Progressive Muscle Relaxation:**
   - Practice progressive muscle relaxation by tensing and then releasing muscle groups throughout your body. Start with your toes and work your way up to your head, gradually releasing tension and promoting relaxation.

5. **Mindfulness and Grounding Techniques:**
   - Practice mindfulness techniques to stay present and focused during your presentation. Use grounding techniques, such as focusing on your breath or sensations in your body, to anchor yourself in the present moment and reduce anxiety about the future.

6. **Positive Self-Talk:**
   - Challenge negative self-talk and replace it with positive affirmations. Remind yourself of past successes and strengths, and

focus on your ability to handle the challenges of public speaking. Repeat affirmations such as "I am prepared and capable" or "I am confident in my abilities" to boost your confidence.

7. Focus on the Audience:
- Shift your focus away from yourself and onto the audience. Instead of worrying about how you're perceived, focus on delivering value to your audience and meeting their needs. Engage with audience members through eye contact, gestures, and interactive elements to build rapport and connection.

8. Use Humor and Personal Stories:
- Incorporate humor and personal stories into your presentation to lighten the mood and create a more relaxed atmosphere. Sharing relatable anecdotes can humanize you as a speaker and help you connect with your audience on a personal level.

9. Accept Imperfection:
- Accept that it's normal to feel nervous before speaking in public. Embrace imperfection and recognize that mistakes or minor setbacks are part of the learning process. Shift your focus from perfection to authenticity and genuine connection with your audience.

10. Seek Support and Feedback:
- Seek support from friends, family, or colleagues who can provide encouragement and constructive feedback. Practice speaking in front of a supportive audience or join a public speaking group to gain valuable experience and confidence.

Visualization and Positive Affirmations

Visualization and positive affirmations are powerful techniques for overcoming public speaking anxiety and building confidence in your speaking abilities. Here's how you can use them effectively:

1. Visualization:

- Find a quiet and comfortable space where you won't be disturbed. Close your eyes and imagine yourself giving a successful presentation in vivid detail.
- Visualize the venue, the audience, and yourself standing confidently on stage. Picture yourself speaking with clarity, confidence, and poise.
- Engage all your senses in the visualization process. Imagine the sound of your voice, the expressions on the audience's faces, and the feeling of confidence and empowerment coursing through your body.
- Visualize the audience responding positively to your message, nodding in agreement, and applauding at the end of your presentation.
- Practice visualization regularly, ideally daily, leading up to your presentation. The more vivid and detailed your visualization, the more effective it will be in reducing anxiety and boosting confidence.

2. Positive Affirmations:
- Create a list of positive affirmations related to public speaking and confidence. These affirmations should be personalized to address any specific fears or insecurities you may have.
- Examples of positive affirmations include:
  - "I am a confident and effective speaker."
  - "I am well-prepared and capable of delivering a successful presentation."
  - "I am excited to share my message with the audience."
  - "I trust in my ability to handle any challenges that may arise during my presentation."
- Repeat these affirmations to yourself regularly, especially before and during moments of anxiety or self-doubt. Say them aloud with conviction, and visualize them as true statements about yourself.
- Write your affirmations on sticky notes or index cards and place them in visible locations where you'll see them frequently, such as your desk, mirror, or computer screen.

3. Combine Visualization with Affirmations:
- Combine visualization with positive affirmations for maximum effectiveness. Before you begin your visualization practice, recite your affirmations aloud to yourself.
- As you visualize yourself giving a successful presentation, reinforce your positive affirmations in your mind. Repeat them silently as you imagine yourself speaking confidently and engaging with the audience.

- Use the power of visualization to anchor the affirmations in your subconscious mind, reinforcing your belief in your abilities and reducing anxiety.

4. Practice Consistently:

- Consistency is key to seeing results with visualization and positive affirmations. Make them a regular part of your daily routine, especially in the days leading up to your presentation.
- Set aside dedicated time each day for visualization and affirmation practice. Even just a few minutes of focused practice can make a significant difference in reducing anxiety and increasing confidence.

Turning Nervous Energy into Dynamic Delivery

Turning nervous energy into dynamic delivery is a valuable skill that can help you harness the adrenaline and excitement of public speaking to enhance your performance. Here's how you can channel nervous energy into a powerful and engaging presentation:

1. Reframe Nervousness as Excitement:

- Instead of viewing nervousness as a negative emotion, reframe it as excitement. Recognize that the adrenaline rush you feel before speaking in public is your body's natural response to a challenging and exhilarating opportunity.
- Embrace the energy and enthusiasm that comes with nervousness, and channel it into your presentation to fuel your passion and engagement with the audience.

2. Use Physical Movement:

- Incorporate purposeful physical movement into your presentation to release nervous energy and engage your audience. Move around the stage with confidence, use expressive gestures to emphasize key points, and vary your body language to keep the audience's attention.
- Avoid pacing back and forth nervously or fidgeting with objects, as this can be distracting. Instead, use intentional movement to command the stage and captivate your audience.

3. Practice Controlled Breathing:

- Practice deep breathing exercises to calm your nerves and regulate your breathing before and during your presentation. Take slow, deep breaths from your diaphragm to relax your body and center your mind.
- Use controlled breathing techniques, such as inhaling deeply for a count of four, holding your breath for a count of four, and exhaling slowly for a count of four, to reduce anxiety and promote relaxation.

4. Focus on Audience Engagement:
- Shift your focus away from your own nervousness and onto engaging with your audience. Make eye contact with individual audience members, smile, and convey enthusiasm and passion for your topic.
- Actively involve the audience in your presentation through questions, interactive activities, or storytelling. Engaging with the audience can help distract you from your nerves and create a more dynamic and interactive presentation.

5. Embrace Imperfection:
- Accept that it's normal to feel nervous before speaking in public, and recognize that imperfection is part of the human experience. Instead of striving for flawless performance, focus on connecting authentically with your audience and delivering your message with sincerity and passion.
- Embrace mistakes as opportunities for learning and growth, and don't let fear of imperfection hold you back from giving your best effort.

6. Visualize Success:
- Visualize yourself delivering a successful and impactful presentation with confidence and poise. Imagine the audience responding positively to your message, nodding in agreement, and engaging with you throughout your presentation.
- Use visualization techniques to mentally rehearse your presentation, focusing on positive outcomes and reinforcing your belief in your ability to overcome nervousness and deliver a dynamic delivery.

7. Practice, Practice, Practice:
- The more you practice your presentation, the more comfortable and confident you'll become. Rehearse your speech multiple times,

preferably in front of a mirror or with a trusted friend or colleague who can provide feedback.

- Practice speaking in front of different audiences to desensitize yourself to the nerves associated with public speaking. Each successful experience will boost your confidence and reduce anxiety over time.

Seeking Professional Help for Persistent Anxiety

Seeking professional help for persistent public speaking anxiety is a proactive step towards overcoming this challenge and becoming a more confident and effective speaker. Here's how you can approach seeking professional assistance:

1. **Recognize When to Seek Help:**
   - If you experience persistent and debilitating anxiety or fear related to public speaking that significantly impacts your personal or professional life, it may be time to seek professional help.
   - Signs that indicate you may benefit from professional assistance include overwhelming anxiety before speaking engagements, avoidance of public speaking opportunities, difficulty functioning due to anxiety, and negative impacts on your self-esteem or career advancement.

2. **Research Mental Health Professionals:**
   - Start by researching mental health professionals who specialize in treating anxiety disorders, including public speaking anxiety. Look for therapists, counselors, or psychologists who have experience working with individuals with similar challenges.
   - Consider seeking professionals who offer cognitive-behavioral therapy (CBT), exposure therapy, or other evidence-based treatments for anxiety disorders, as these approaches have been shown to be effective for managing public speaking anxiety.

3. **Ask for Recommendations:**
   - Reach out to trusted friends, family members, or colleagues who have sought therapy for anxiety or mental health issues. Ask for recommendations or referrals to mental health professionals they trust and have had positive experiences with.

- Consider seeking recommendations from healthcare providers, such as your primary care physician or a psychiatrist, who may be able to refer you to qualified mental health professionals in your area.

4. Schedule an Initial Consultation:

- Once you've identified potential mental health professionals, schedule an initial consultation or appointment to discuss your concerns and determine if they're a good fit for your needs.
- Use the initial consultation as an opportunity to ask questions, share your experiences with public speaking anxiety, and learn more about the therapist's approach to treatment. Pay attention to factors such as rapport, communication style, and expertise in treating anxiety disorders.

5. Discuss Treatment Options:

- During your initial consultation, discuss treatment options for addressing public speaking anxiety. Your therapist may recommend individual therapy, group therapy, or a combination of approaches based on your specific needs and preferences.
- Be open to exploring different treatment modalities, such as cognitive-behavioral therapy (CBT), exposure therapy, relaxation techniques, mindfulness-based interventions, or medication management, depending on your situation and the severity of your anxiety.

6. Commit to Treatment:

- If you decide to pursue therapy for public speaking anxiety, commit to attending regular therapy sessions and actively participating in the therapeutic process. Be honest and open with your therapist about your experiences, thoughts, and feelings related to public speaking anxiety.
- Follow your therapist's recommendations for homework assignments, coping strategies, and practice exercises outside of therapy sessions to maximize the effectiveness of treatment.

7. Monitor Progress and Adjust as Needed:

- Monitor your progress in therapy and communicate openly with your therapist about any changes or challenges you experience. Be patient and persistent, as overcoming public speaking anxiety is a gradual process that may require time and effort.

- If you're not making progress or experiencing significant distress despite therapy, discuss alternative treatment options with your therapist, such as medication adjustments, referral to a specialist, or additional support services.

8. Practice Self-Care:
- In addition to seeking professional help, practice self-care techniques to manage stress and anxiety related to public speaking. Get regular exercise, prioritize adequate sleep, practice relaxation techniques, maintain a healthy lifestyle, and engage in activities that bring you joy and fulfillment.

9. Stay Committed to Growth:
- Overcoming public speaking anxiety is a journey of growth and self-discovery. Stay committed to your personal development and celebrate your progress, no matter how small. Be kind and compassionate to yourself as you navigate the challenges of public speaking anxiety.

Chapter 8
Preparation and Rehearsal Techniques

Developing a Pre-Speech Routine

Developing a pre-speech routine can help you prepare mentally and physically for public speaking, increasing your confidence and performance on stage. Here's how to create an effective pre-speech routine:

1. **Set Clear Objectives:**
   - Before developing your routine, clarify your objectives for the speech. Determine what you want to achieve, whether it's informing, persuading, entertaining, or inspiring your audience. Understanding your goals will guide your preparation and rehearsal process.

2. **Visualize Success:**
   - Visualize yourself delivering a successful presentation. Imagine yourself speaking confidently, engaging the audience, and receiving positive feedback. Visualizing success can boost your confidence and reduce anxiety before speaking.

3. **Review and Memorize Key Points:**
   - Review your speech outline or notes to ensure you're familiar with the content. Focus on memorizing key points, transitions, and important details. Practice reciting your speech aloud to reinforce your memory and build fluency.

4. **Practice Relaxation Techniques:**
   - Incorporate relaxation techniques into your routine to calm nerves and reduce anxiety. Practice deep breathing, progressive muscle relaxation, or visualization exercises to relax your body and mind before speaking.

5. **Warm Up Your Voice and Body:**
   - Warm up your voice and body to prepare for speaking. Perform vocal warm-up exercises to loosen your vocal cords and improve articulation. Stretch or engage in light physical activity to release tension and increase blood flow.

6. **Review Technical Setup:**

- Review the technical setup and logistics of your presentation venue. Ensure that audiovisual equipment, microphones, lighting, and any other technical aspects are functioning properly. Familiarize yourself with the layout of the stage and any props or visual aids you'll be using.

7. Practice Positive Affirmations:
- Use positive affirmations to boost your confidence and mindset before speaking. Repeat affirmations such as "I am prepared and capable," "I am confident in my abilities," or "I am excited to share my message with the audience" to reinforce positive self-talk.

8. Visualize Audience Engagement:
- Visualize yourself engaging with the audience and delivering your message with impact. Imagine the audience responding positively to your presentation, nodding in agreement, and actively participating in the discussion. Visualizing audience engagement can help you connect with your listeners and feel more comfortable on stage.

9. Stay Hydrated and Energized:
- Drink water and eat a light, nutritious snack to stay hydrated and energized before speaking. Avoid consuming caffeine or sugary foods, as they can increase anxiety and jitteriness. Choose foods that provide sustained energy and focus, such as fruits, nuts, or whole grains.

10. Arrive Early and Review Materials:
- Arrive at the venue early to acclimate to the environment and review your materials. Take time to walk around the space, familiarize yourself with the stage and seating arrangement, and mentally prepare for speaking. Review your speech notes or visual aids one final time to ensure readiness.

11. Find a Quiet Moment for Focus:
- Find a quiet moment before speaking to center yourself and focus on the task ahead. Take a few minutes to gather your thoughts, visualize success, and mentally rehearse your opening lines. Use this time to cultivate a positive and confident mindset before taking the stage.

12. Practice Gratitude and Positivity:

- Practice gratitude and positivity as part of your pre-speech routine. Reflect on the opportunity to share your message with others and express gratitude for the chance to connect with your audience. Cultivating a mindset of gratitude can help shift your focus away from fear and anxiety towards appreciation and excitement.

Effective Speech Outlining and Scripting

Creating an effective speech outline and scripting your presentation are essential steps in preparing for public speaking engagements. Here's how to develop a structured and compelling speech outline:

1. **Understand Your Purpose and Audience:**
   - Clarify the purpose of your speech and identify your target audience. Determine what you want to achieve with your presentation and tailor your content to meet the needs and interests of your audience.

2. **Choose a Clear Structure:**
   - Select a clear and logical structure for your speech. Common structures include chronological (time-based), topical (theme-based), problem-solution, cause-effect, or spatial (location-based) organization. Choose the structure that best suits your topic and objectives.

3. **Craft a Strong Opening:**
   - Begin your speech with a captivating opening that grabs the audience's attention and sets the tone for your presentation. Consider using a compelling anecdote, surprising statistic, provocative question, or powerful quote to pique interest and engage listeners from the start.

4. **Outline Main Points:**
   - Outline the main points or key ideas you want to convey in your speech. These main points should support your overarching message and flow logically from one to the next. Use bullet points or numbered lists to organize your ideas in a clear and concise manner.

5. Provide Supporting Evidence and Examples:

- Support each main point with relevant evidence, examples, statistics, or anecdotes to strengthen your argument and provide context for your audience. Use credible sources and real-life examples to add depth and credibility to your presentation.

6. Include Transitions:

- Use transitions to smoothly guide your audience from one point to the next and maintain coherence throughout your speech. Transitional phrases or sentences can signal shifts in topic, reinforce connections between ideas, and help the audience follow your train of thought.

7. Anticipate Counterarguments:

- Anticipate potential counterarguments or objections your audience may have and address them preemptively in your speech. Acknowledging opposing viewpoints demonstrates credibility and shows that you've considered multiple perspectives.

8. Craft a Memorable Closing:

- Conclude your speech with a memorable closing that reinforces your main message and leaves a lasting impression on your audience. Summarize key points, reiterate your main message, and end with a strong call to action, thought-provoking statement, or memorable quote.

9. Consider Speech Length:

- Consider the time allotted for your speech and adjust the length and depth of your content accordingly. Aim for a balance between providing sufficient information and maintaining audience engagement within the time constraints.

10. Practice Delivery:

- Practice delivering your speech with your outline and script, focusing on clarity, pacing, and emphasis. Familiarize yourself with the flow of your presentation and rehearse transitions between key points to ensure smooth delivery.

11. Seek Feedback:

- Seek feedback from trusted colleagues, mentors, or friends on your speech outline and script. Ask for constructive criticism and suggestions for improvement, and be open to making revisions based on feedback.

12. Revise and Refine:
   - Revise and refine your speech outline and script based on feedback and personal reflection. Edit for clarity, coherence, and conciseness, ensuring that every word contributes to your overall message and enhances audience understanding.

Rehearsing for Flow and Natural Delivery

Rehearsing for flow and natural delivery is crucial for ensuring that your public speaking presentations are engaging, polished, and confidently delivered. Here are some effective techniques to rehearse your speech for flow and naturalness:

1. Memorize Key Points, Not Entire Script:
   - Instead of memorizing your entire speech word-for-word, focus on memorizing key points, main ideas, and transitions. This allows for more flexibility and spontaneity in your delivery, making it feel more natural and conversational.

2. Use Visual Aids Sparingly:
   - If you're using visual aids such as slides or props, rehearse your speech with them to ensure smooth integration into your presentation. However, avoid over-relying on visual aids, as they can detract from your natural delivery if you become too dependent on them.

3. Practice Pacing and Timing:
   - Pay attention to pacing and timing during rehearsals to ensure that you're not speaking too quickly or too slowly. Practice delivering your speech at a comfortable and steady pace, pausing for emphasis and allowing time for audience engagement.

4. Record Yourself:
   - Record yourself rehearsing your speech and listen or watch the playback to identify areas for improvement. Pay attention to your tone

of voice, body language, and overall delivery, and make adjustments as needed to enhance flow and naturalness.

5. Focus on Expression and Emotion:
- Infuse your delivery with expression and emotion to engage your audience and convey authenticity. Practice varying your tone of voice, facial expressions, and gestures to match the content of your speech and connect with your audience on a deeper level.

6. Practice Active Listening:
- Practice active listening during rehearsals by imagining yourself as a member of the audience. Listen attentively to your own delivery, paying attention to how it sounds and feels from the perspective of the listener. This can help you identify areas where you may need to adjust your delivery for clarity or impact.

7. Rehearse in Different Settings:
- Rehearse your speech in different settings and environments to simulate the conditions of your actual presentation. Practice in front of a mirror, in an empty room, or with a small group of friends or colleagues to build confidence and adaptability in various speaking situations.

8. Seek Feedback and Rehearse Again:
- Seek feedback from trusted colleagues, mentors, or friends after rehearsing your speech. Ask for constructive criticism on your delivery, flow, and naturalness, and use their feedback to make further adjustments and refinements.

9. Be Yourself:
- Above all, be yourself when rehearsing and delivering your speech. Embrace your unique personality, style, and voice, and let your authentic self shine through in your presentation. Authenticity fosters connection and trust with your audience, leading to a more engaging and impactful delivery.

10. Stay Flexible and Adapt:
- While it's important to rehearse for flow and natural delivery, it's also essential to stay flexible and adapt to unexpected changes or

challenges during your actual presentation. Trust in your preparation and rehearsal process, and have confidence in your ability to deliver your message effectively in any situation.

Conducting Mock Presentations for Feedback

Conducting mock presentations for feedback is a valuable rehearsal technique that can help you refine your public speaking skills, gain valuable insights, and improve your overall performance. Here's how to effectively conduct mock presentations and leverage feedback for improvement:

1. **Select Your Audience:**
   - Choose a small group of trusted colleagues, friends, or mentors to serve as your audience for the mock presentation. Ideally, select individuals who can provide constructive feedback and perspective on your speech delivery, content, and overall effectiveness.

2. **Set the Stage:**
   - Create a presentation environment that closely resembles the actual setting of your upcoming speech. Set up any necessary equipment, such as a podium, microphone, or visual aids, and arrange seating to mimic the layout of the audience. This helps you simulate the experience of delivering your speech in a realistic setting.

3. **Deliver Your Presentation:**
   - Deliver your speech to the mock audience as you would during the actual presentation. Practice your delivery, pacing, and gestures, and strive for a confident and engaging performance. Focus on connecting with your audience and effectively conveying your message.

4. **Encourage Feedback:**
   - After completing your presentation, invite members of the mock audience to provide feedback on various aspects of your speech. Encourage honest and constructive feedback on areas such as content, delivery, body language, vocal tone, clarity, and overall effectiveness.
   - Provide specific prompts or questions to guide feedback, such as:
     - "What did you find most compelling about the presentation?"

- "Were there any parts of the speech that were unclear or confusing?"
  - "How could I improve my delivery or body language?"
  - "Did the visual aids effectively support the message?"

5. Listen Actively:
- Listen actively to the feedback provided by members of the mock audience. Pay attention to both positive feedback and areas for improvement, and be open to constructive criticism. Take notes on the feedback to capture key insights and suggestions for enhancement.

6. Reflect and Analyze:
- Take time to reflect on the feedback received and analyze areas where you can make improvements. Consider how the feedback aligns with your own perceptions of your presentation and identify patterns or recurring themes in the feedback.
- Be honest with yourself about areas where you may need to make adjustments or changes to enhance your performance.

7. Implement Changes:
- Based on the feedback received, make targeted adjustments to your speech content, delivery, and presentation style. Incorporate suggestions for improvement into your rehearsal process and practice implementing changes until they become natural and seamless.
- Experiment with different techniques and strategies to address feedback, such as adjusting your pacing, refining your transitions, enhancing your vocal variety, or refining your visual aids.

8. Rehearse Again:
- Rehearse your revised presentation multiple times to integrate feedback and ensure that you're comfortable with the changes. Practice delivering your speech with confidence and conviction, focusing on maintaining a natural and engaging delivery style.

9. Seek Additional Feedback:
- If possible, conduct additional mock presentations or seek feedback from different audiences to gather diverse perspectives and insights. Each round of feedback can provide new opportunities for growth and refinement.

10. **Express Gratitude:**
   - Express gratitude to the members of your mock audience for their time, attention, and feedback. Acknowledge the value of their insights and contributions to your growth as a speaker, and let them know that their feedback is appreciated and taken seriously.

Preparing for Unexpected Challenges During Speech

Preparing for unexpected challenges during a speech is crucial for maintaining composure, confidence, and effectiveness as a speaker. Here are some practical techniques to help you anticipate and address potential challenges:

1. **Know Your Material Inside and Out:**
   - Thoroughly familiarize yourself with your speech content, main points, key messages, and supporting evidence. The more you know your material, the better equipped you'll be to adapt to unexpected challenges or disruptions.

2. **Prepare for Technical Issues:**
   - Anticipate technical challenges that may arise, such as malfunctioning audiovisual equipment, microphone problems, or issues with slides or visual aids. Have a backup plan in place, such as printed copies of your slides or notes, and be prepared to continue your presentation even if technical difficulties occur.

3. **Practice Improvisation:**
   - Practice improvisational speaking techniques to handle unexpected interruptions or distractions gracefully. Develop the ability to think on your feet, respond spontaneously to audience questions or comments, and adapt your speech on the spot if necessary.

4. **Rehearse Under Different Conditions:**
   - Rehearse your speech under different conditions to simulate potential challenges or distractions. Practice speaking in noisy

environments, with interruptions, or in unfamiliar settings to build resilience and adaptability as a speaker.

5. Visualize Success:
- Visualize yourself successfully navigating unexpected challenges during your speech. Mentally rehearse how you will handle various scenarios with confidence, poise, and professionalism. Visualizing success can help reduce anxiety and increase your readiness to address challenges in the moment.

6. Maintain a Positive Mindset:
- Cultivate a positive mindset and attitude towards unexpected challenges. Instead of viewing them as obstacles or setbacks, see them as opportunities for growth, learning, and demonstrating resilience as a speaker. Embrace the challenge with confidence and optimism.

7. Stay Calm and Centered:
- Practice relaxation techniques, such as deep breathing or mindfulness meditation, to stay calm and centered before and during your speech. Remind yourself to stay present in the moment and focus on delivering your message effectively, regardless of any unexpected challenges that may arise.

8. Engage the Audience:
- Use audience engagement techniques to maintain connection and interest during your speech, even in the face of unexpected challenges. Encourage participation, ask questions, or use humor to keep the audience engaged and attentive.

9. Be Flexible and Adaptable:
- Stay flexible and adaptable in your approach to speaking, especially when unexpected challenges occur. Be prepared to adjust your speech delivery, timing, or content as needed to accommodate changing circumstances and keep the presentation on track.

10. Practice Resilience:
- Develop resilience as a speaker by embracing failure, setbacks, and challenges as opportunities for growth and improvement. Learn from each experience, reflect on what went well and what could be

improved, and use that knowledge to become a more effective and confident speaker in the future.

11. **Seek Support if Needed:**
   - If unexpected challenges during your speech become overwhelming or unmanageable, don't hesitate to seek support from event organizers, technical staff, or trusted colleagues. Asking for assistance when needed demonstrates resourcefulness and professionalism as a speaker.

Chapter 9
Handling
Challenging
Situations

Dealing with Technical Difficulties

Dealing with technical difficulties during a public speaking engagement can be daunting, but with preparation and a calm demeanor, you can handle these challenges effectively. Here's how to navigate technical difficulties with confidence:

1. **Prepare in Advance:**
   - Familiarize yourself with the technical setup and equipment you'll be using before your presentation. Visit the venue early, test the microphone, audiovisual equipment, and any other technology to ensure everything is functioning properly.

2. **Have a Backup Plan:**
   - Always have a backup plan in case of technical failures. Carry backup copies of your presentation on a USB drive or have printed handouts available. Consider memorizing key points of your speech in case you need to proceed without visual aids.

3. **Stay Calm and Composed:**
   - If technical difficulties arise during your presentation, stay calm and composed. Panicking or becoming flustered will only escalate the situation and undermine your credibility as a speaker. Take a deep breath, maintain a positive attitude, and focus on finding a solution.

4. **Troubleshoot Quickly:**
   - Quickly assess the nature of the technical issue and attempt to troubleshoot it if possible. Check connections, cables, and settings to identify the source of the problem. If you're unable to resolve the issue yourself, seek assistance from event organizers or technical support staff.

5. **Communicate with the Audience:**
   - Transparently communicate the technical difficulties to the audience in a calm and professional manner. Let them know that you're experiencing technical issues and reassure them that you're working to resolve the problem. Apologize for the inconvenience and thank them for their patience.

6. Engage the Audience:

- Use the opportunity to engage with the audience while technical issues are being addressed. Ask questions, share anecdotes, or initiate a discussion to keep the audience engaged and maintain momentum until the problem is resolved.

7. Maintain Eye Contact:

- Maintain eye contact with the audience while addressing technical difficulties. This demonstrates confidence and keeps the audience focused on you rather than the technical issues. Use gestures and facial expressions to convey assurance and maintain connection with the audience.

8. Keep Your Presentation Concise:

- If technical difficulties persist and time is limited, consider condensing your presentation to focus on key points or critical information. Adapt your speech on the fly to accommodate the situation and ensure that you deliver the most essential content within the available time.

9. Stay Flexible and Adapt:

- Stay flexible and adaptable in your approach to the presentation. Be prepared to adjust your delivery, pacing, or content based on the evolving circumstances. Embrace the challenge as an opportunity to demonstrate your resilience and professionalism as a speaker.

10. Resume with Confidence:

- Once the technical issues have been resolved, resume your presentation with confidence. Quickly regain the audience's attention and smoothly transition back into your speech. Use humor or a brief recap to re-engage the audience and refocus their attention on your message.

11. Seek Feedback Afterwards:

- After your presentation, seek feedback from event organizers, technical staff, or audience members on how the technical difficulties were handled. Use their insights to learn from the experience and improve your preparedness for future speaking engagements.

Addressing Unexpected Questions

Addressing unexpected questions during a public speaking engagement requires quick thinking, confidence, and effective communication skills. Here's how to handle unexpected questions with poise and professionalism:

1. **Stay Calm and Confident:**
   - Maintain a calm and confident demeanor when faced with unexpected questions. Remind yourself that it's normal to receive questions, and view them as an opportunity to engage with the audience and demonstrate your expertise on the topic.

2. **Listen Carefully:**
   - Listen attentively to the question being asked, ensuring that you fully understand its content and context. If necessary, ask the audience member to repeat or clarify the question to ensure clarity before responding.

3. **Pause and Reflect:**
   - Take a brief pause to collect your thoughts and formulate a thoughtful response to the question. Avoid rushing into an answer without considering the question carefully, as this can lead to misunderstandings or incomplete responses.

4. **Acknowledge and Validate:**
   - Acknowledge the audience member who asked the question and thank them for their contribution to the discussion. Validate their question by expressing appreciation for their curiosity or insight, even if the question is challenging or unexpected.

5. **Repeat or Paraphrase:**
   - Repeat or paraphrase the question to ensure that everyone in the audience understands what was asked. This also provides you with a moment to internalize the question and formulate your response more effectively.

6. **Be Honest and Transparent:**

- Be honest and transparent in your response, even if you don't have a ready-made answer to the question. If you're unsure or don't know the answer, it's okay to admit it rather than attempting to bluff or provide inaccurate information.

7. Draw on Your Knowledge and Experience:

- Draw on your knowledge, expertise, and personal experiences to craft a well-informed response to the question. Share relevant insights, examples, or anecdotes that demonstrate your understanding of the topic and add value to your response.

8. Stay on Topic:

- Stay focused on the topic at hand and avoid going off on tangents or getting sidetracked by unrelated issues. Keep your response concise and relevant to the question being asked to maintain clarity and coherence.

9. Encourage Dialogue:

- Encourage dialogue and interaction with the audience by inviting follow-up questions or comments after providing your initial response. Engage in a respectful and open exchange of ideas to foster a dynamic and enriching discussion.

10. Remain Respectful and Professional:

- Maintain a respectful and professional tone when responding to unexpected questions, even if they are challenging or critical in nature. Avoid becoming defensive or confrontational, and respond to questions with patience, empathy, and understanding.

11. Redirect if Necessary:

- If a question is unrelated to the topic or inappropriate for the context of the presentation, politely redirect the conversation back to the main topic or offer to discuss the issue further offline after the presentation.

12. Follow Up if Needed:

- If you're unable to fully address a complex or nuanced question during the presentation, offer to follow up with the audience member afterward to provide more information or clarification. This demonstrates your commitment to addressing their concerns and fostering ongoing engagement.

Managing Disruptions and Unexpected Events

Managing disruptions and unexpected events during a public speaking engagement requires quick thinking, adaptability, and a calm demeanor. Here's how to handle such situations effectively:

1. **Stay Calm and Composed:**
   - Maintain a calm and composed demeanor when faced with disruptions or unexpected events. Take a deep breath to center yourself and remind yourself that it's normal for unforeseen circumstances to arise during public speaking engagements.

2. **Assess the Situation Quickly:**
   - Assess the nature and severity of the disruption or unexpected event as quickly as possible. Determine whether it's something that can be addressed immediately or if it requires a more nuanced response.

3. **Address the Issue Promptly:**
   - Address the disruption or unexpected event promptly and decisively. Depending on the situation, this may involve pausing your presentation momentarily to acknowledge the issue, providing guidance to the audience, or taking action to mitigate the impact of the disruption.

4. **Maintain Control of the Room:**
   - Assert control of the room and establish yourself as the leader in managing the situation. Use a confident and authoritative tone of voice to command attention and reassure the audience that you're in control.

5. **Communicate Transparently:**
   - Communicate transparently with the audience about the nature of the disruption or unexpected event. Provide clear and concise information about what's happening and any steps being taken to address the issue.

6. Adapt Your Approach:
   - Be prepared to adapt your approach to the presentation in response to disruptions or unexpected events. This may involve modifying your delivery, adjusting the content of your speech, or changing the format of the presentation as needed.

7. Maintain Flexibility:
   - Stay flexible and open-minded in your response to disruptions or unexpected events. Be willing to deviate from your original plan if necessary to accommodate the situation and ensure the safety and well-being of everyone involved.

8. Engage the Audience:
   - Engage the audience in the process of managing the disruption or unexpected event, if appropriate. Encourage participation, ask for assistance if needed, and foster a sense of community and cooperation among attendees.

9. Stay Positive and Resilient:
   - Maintain a positive and resilient attitude in the face of disruptions or unexpected events. Focus on finding solutions rather than dwelling on the problem, and demonstrate confidence and optimism in your ability to overcome challenges.

10. Seek Assistance if Necessary:
   - If the disruption or unexpected event is beyond your ability to manage alone, don't hesitate to seek assistance from event organizers, venue staff, or relevant authorities. Collaborate with others to address the issue effectively and ensure the safety and well-being of everyone involved.

11. Resume the Presentation Smoothly:
   - Once the disruption or unexpected event has been addressed, resume the presentation smoothly and seamlessly. Transition back into your speech with confidence and professionalism, using techniques such as humor or a brief recap to re-engage the audience and refocus their attention.

12. Reflect and Learn:

- After the presentation, take time to reflect on how the disruption or unexpected event was handled and identify any lessons learned. Consider what went well and what could be improved for future speaking engagements, and use the experience as an opportunity for growth and development.

Navigating Controversial Topics

Navigating controversial topics during a public speaking engagement requires sensitivity, preparation, and effective communication skills. Here's how to handle such situations with confidence and professionalism:

1. **Know Your Audience:**
   - Understand the demographics, perspectives, and sensitivities of your audience before addressing controversial topics. Tailor your message and approach to resonate with your audience's values, beliefs, and level of tolerance for contentious issues.

2. **Research Thoroughly:**
   - Conduct thorough research on the controversial topic you'll be addressing, including different viewpoints, arguments, and evidence surrounding the issue. Familiarize yourself with relevant facts, statistics, and historical context to support your arguments and provide context for your audience.

3. **Clarify Your Position:**
   - Clarify your position on the controversial topic and articulate it clearly and confidently to your audience. Clearly state your stance, rationale, and perspective on the issue, and be prepared to defend your position with reasoned arguments and evidence.

4. **Acknowledge Different Perspectives:**
   - Acknowledge and respect the diversity of perspectives and opinions that may exist within your audience. Recognize that controversial topics often evoke strong emotions and differing viewpoints, and strive to foster a respectful and inclusive dialogue that acknowledges and validates diverse perspectives.

5. Encourage Constructive Dialogue:

- Encourage constructive dialogue and open exchange of ideas among audience members during the discussion of controversial topics. Create a safe and inclusive environment where individuals feel comfortable expressing their opinions and engaging in meaningful dialogue with others.

6. Remain Neutral and Impartial:

- Maintain a neutral and impartial stance when discussing controversial topics, especially if you're serving as a moderator or facilitator of a panel discussion or debate. Avoid expressing personal biases or taking sides on the issue, and strive to facilitate a balanced and fair discussion among participants.

7. Use Empathetic Communication:

- Practice empathetic communication when addressing controversial topics, showing empathy and understanding for the perspectives and experiences of others, even if you disagree with them. Use language that is respectful, non-confrontational, and empathetic to foster connection and empathy with your audience.

8. Manage Emotions Effectively:

- Manage your own emotions effectively when discussing controversial topics, especially if the discussion becomes heated or emotionally charged. Stay composed, composed, and level-headed, and avoid reacting impulsively or defensively to emotional responses from the audience.

9. Set Ground Rules for Discussion:

- Establish clear ground rules for discussion to ensure that the conversation remains respectful, constructive, and focused on the issues at hand. Set expectations for civility, active listening, and mutual respect among participants, and enforce these rules as needed to maintain a productive dialogue.

10. Address Misinformation and Misconceptions:

- Address misinformation and misconceptions about the controversial topic with factual information and evidence-based arguments. Correct inaccuracies or misunderstandings politely but firmly, and provide accurate information to clarify any confusion or misunderstanding.

11. Seek Common Ground:

- Look for opportunities to identify and emphasize areas of common ground or shared values among participants, even on contentious issues. Highlighting shared values or goals can help bridge divides and foster understanding and collaboration among individuals with differing perspectives.

12. Conclude on a Positive Note:

- Conclude the discussion of controversial topics on a positive note by summarizing key points, highlighting areas of agreement or consensus, and expressing optimism for continued dialogue and progress on the issue. Reinforce the importance of respectful dialogue and constructive engagement in addressing complex and divisive issues.

Staying Calm and Composed in Difficult Situations

Staying calm and composed in difficult situations is essential for maintaining credibility, confidence, and effectiveness as a public speaker. Here are some strategies to help you remain poised and collected when faced with challenging situations during public speaking engagements:

1. Practice Relaxation Techniques:

- Incorporate relaxation techniques such as deep breathing, mindfulness meditation, or progressive muscle relaxation into your routine to help manage stress and anxiety. Practice these techniques regularly to build resilience and maintain a sense of calmness in difficult situations.

2. Visualize Success:

- Visualize yourself successfully navigating challenging situations during public speaking engagements. Mentally rehearse how you will remain calm, composed, and confident in the face of adversity, and visualize yourself delivering your message with poise and professionalism.

3. Focus on the Present Moment:

   - Stay focused on the present moment rather than dwelling on past mistakes or worrying about future outcomes. Focus on the task at hand and channel your energy into delivering your message effectively, regardless of any distractions or challenges that may arise.

4. Maintain Perspective:

   - Keep things in perspective and remind yourself that setbacks or challenges during public speaking engagements are a normal part of the process. Approach difficult situations with a growth mindset, viewing them as opportunities for learning, growth, and personal development.

5. Prepare Thoroughly:

   - Thoroughly prepare for your public speaking engagements to build confidence and reduce anxiety. Rehearse your speech multiple times, anticipate potential challenges or objections, and prepare responses to address them effectively. The more prepared you are, the more confident and composed you'll feel during the presentation.

6. Stay Flexible and Adaptable:

   - Embrace flexibility and adaptability in your approach to public speaking. Be prepared to adjust your presentation style, content, or delivery based on the needs and reactions of the audience, as well as any unexpected developments that may occur during the presentation.

7. Practice Positive Self-Talk:

   - Practice positive self-talk to boost your confidence and self-esteem before and during public speaking engagements. Replace negative thoughts or self-doubt with affirmations and empowering statements that reinforce your abilities and strengths as a speaker.

8. Use Humor Appropriately:

   - Use humor appropriately to lighten the mood and diffuse tension during difficult situations. Injecting a touch of humor into your presentation can help you connect with the audience, alleviate stress, and create a more positive and engaging atmosphere.

9. Maintain Professionalism:

- Maintain professionalism at all times, even when faced with challenging situations or difficult audience members. Stay composed, courteous, and respectful in your interactions, and avoid reacting impulsively or emotionally to provocation or criticism.

10. Seek Support if Needed:

- Don't hesitate to seek support from event organizers, colleagues, or mentors if you're feeling overwhelmed or unsure how to handle a difficult situation. Asking for assistance demonstrates resourcefulness and a commitment to delivering a successful presentation.

11. Reflect and Learn:

- After the public speaking engagement, take time to reflect on your performance and how you handled any challenging situations that arose. Identify areas for improvement and consider what you can learn from the experience to enhance your skills and confidence as a speaker.

Chapter 10
Engaging and Persuasive Delivery

The Importance of Engaging Your Audience

Engaging your audience is crucial for effective public speaking, as it not only captures their attention but also keeps them interested, involved, and receptive to your message. Here's why engaging your audience is important:

1. Capturing Attention:
   - Engaging your audience from the start helps capture their attention and encourages them to focus on your presentation. By using compelling stories, intriguing questions, or attention-grabbing visuals, you can pique their interest and draw them into your message.

2. Maintaining Interest:
   - Keeping your audience engaged throughout your presentation ensures that they remain attentive and receptive to your message. By incorporating variety, such as humor, anecdotes, or interactive elements, you can prevent boredom and maintain their interest from beginning to end.

3. Enhancing Understanding:
   - Engaging presentations are more effective at conveying complex or abstract concepts in a way that is easy to understand and retain. By using relatable examples, vivid imagery, or analogies, you can clarify your message and make it more accessible to your audience.

4. Fostering Connection:
   - Engaging your audience fosters a sense of connection and rapport between you and your listeners. By actively involving them in the presentation through questions, discussions, or interactive activities, you can create a more dynamic and participatory experience that strengthens the bond between speaker and audience.

5. Increasing Retention:
   - Engaging presentations are more memorable and impactful, leading to increased retention of key information. By appealing to multiple senses and emotions, such as sight, sound, and emotion, you can create a lasting impression that resonates with your audience long after the presentation is over.

6. Inspiring Action:
   - Engaging presentations have the power to inspire action and motivate your audience to take the desired next steps. By appealing to their values, beliefs, and emotions, you can influence their attitudes and behaviors in alignment with your message goals.

7. **Building Trust and Credibility:**
   - Engaging your audience demonstrates your competence, confidence, and authenticity as a speaker, building trust and credibility with your listeners. By delivering a well-prepared, engaging presentation, you establish yourself as a knowledgeable and persuasive communicator worth listening to.

8. **Creating a Positive Experience:**
   - Engaging presentations create a positive experience for your audience, leaving them feeling satisfied, entertained, and enlightened. By providing valuable insights, entertainment, or practical takeaways, you leave a lasting impression that reflects positively on you as a speaker.

Techniques for Maintaining Audience Interest

Maintaining audience interest is crucial for effective public speaking, as it ensures that your message is received, understood, and retained. Here are several techniques for keeping your audience engaged and interested throughout your presentation:

1. **Start with a Bang:**
   - Begin your presentation with a strong opening that grabs the audience's attention and sets the tone for the rest of your speech. Use an intriguing fact, a thought-provoking question, a compelling story, or a powerful quote to hook your audience from the start.

2. **Use Varied Content:**
   - Incorporate a variety of content types to keep your audience engaged. Mix spoken words with visuals, such as slides, videos, or props, to appeal to different learning styles and maintain interest.

Break up monotonous sections of speech with interactive elements, such as polls, questions, or group activities, to keep the audience actively involved.

3. Tell Stories:
   - Storytelling is a powerful tool for maintaining audience interest and making your message more relatable and memorable. Use personal anecdotes, case studies, or real-life examples to illustrate key points and evoke emotions that resonate with your audience.

4. Use Humor Wisely:
   - Incorporate humor into your presentation to lighten the mood, engage your audience, and make your message more enjoyable. Use relevant jokes, amusing anecdotes, or witty observations to inject humor into your speech, but be mindful of cultural sensitivities and avoid offensive or inappropriate humor.

5. Involve the Audience:
   - Encourage active participation from your audience to keep them engaged and invested in your presentation. Ask open-ended questions, solicit opinions or experiences, or conduct interactive exercises that encourage audience members to share their thoughts, insights, or reactions.

6. Maintain Eye Contact:
   - Establish and maintain eye contact with your audience throughout your presentation to build rapport, convey confidence, and keep their attention focused on you. Make eye contact with individuals in different sections of the audience to create a sense of connection and inclusivity.

7. Use Vocal Variety:
   - Vary your vocal delivery to keep your audience engaged and interested in your speech. Use changes in pitch, tone, volume, and pace to emphasize key points, convey emotions, and maintain a dynamic and expressive delivery that captures the audience's attention.

8. Keep it Concise:

- Respect your audience's time and attention by keeping your presentation concise and focused on the most essential information. Avoid rambling or going off on tangents, and stick to your main message to ensure that your audience remains engaged and attentive throughout the entire presentation.

9. **Create Visual Impact:**
   - Use visually appealing slides, graphics, or props to enhance the visual impact of your presentation and keep your audience engaged. Choose high-quality images, clear fonts, and simple layouts that support and reinforce your message without overwhelming or distracting your audience.

10. **Inject Passion and Energy:**
   - Infuse your presentation with passion, enthusiasm, and energy to inspire and captivate your audience. Show genuine excitement and conviction about your topic, and let your enthusiasm shine through in your delivery to create a contagious energy that resonates with your audience.

11. **Provide Clear Structure:**
   - Organize your presentation in a clear and logical structure that guides your audience through your main points and keeps them engaged from start to finish. Use signposts, transitions, and summaries to signal key points and help your audience follow the flow of your presentation.

12. **End Strong:**
   - Conclude your presentation with a memorable closing that leaves a lasting impression on your audience. Summarize your key points, reiterate your main message, and leave your audience with a call to action, a thought-provoking question, or a powerful closing statement that reinforces the importance of your message and encourages further reflection or action.

Persuasion Strategies in Public Speaking

Persuasion strategies are essential tools for effective public speaking, allowing speakers to influence and persuade their audience to adopt their ideas, beliefs, or viewpoints. Here are some key persuasion strategies to incorporate into your public speaking:

1. Establish Credibility:

- Establishing credibility is crucial for persuading your audience to trust and believe in your message. Begin by introducing yourself and highlighting your qualifications, expertise, or relevant experience on the topic. Use evidence, such as research findings, testimonials, or personal anecdotes, to support your credibility and reinforce your authority as a speaker.

2. Appeal to Emotions:

- Emotional appeals are powerful persuasion tools that tap into the audience's emotions to evoke empathy, sympathy, or enthusiasm for your message. Use storytelling, vivid imagery, or language that triggers emotional responses to connect with your audience on a deeper level and make your message more compelling and memorable.

3. Use Social Proof:

- Social proof involves leveraging the influence of others to persuade your audience to adopt your viewpoint. Use testimonials, case studies, or examples of successful outcomes to demonstrate how others have benefited from or endorsed your message. Highlighting social proof can build trust and credibility with your audience and make your message more persuasive.

4. Provide Evidence and Logic:

- Providing evidence and logical reasoning is essential for persuading your audience to accept your argument or viewpoint. Present facts, statistics, expert opinions, or logical arguments that support your position and refute counterarguments. Use clear and concise reasoning to demonstrate the validity and soundness of your message and persuade your audience to agree with your perspective.

5. Appeal to Values and Beliefs:

- Appeal to your audience's values, beliefs, and aspirations to make your message more persuasive and relevant to their interests and concerns. Align your message with values that resonate with your audience, such as justice, freedom, or social responsibility, and frame your arguments in a way that appeals to their core beliefs and motivations.

6. Create Contrast and Comparison:

- Creating contrast and comparison can help highlight the benefits or advantages of your message compared to alternatives or opposing viewpoints. Use rhetorical devices such as analogies, metaphors, or contrastive examples to illustrate the differences between your position and others and persuade your audience to choose your viewpoint.

7. Address Counterarguments:

- Anticipate and address potential counterarguments or objections that your audience may have to your message. Acknowledge opposing viewpoints respectfully, but present compelling rebuttals or refutations that undermine the validity of alternative perspectives and reinforce the strength of your argument.

8. Use Persuasive Language:

- Use persuasive language and rhetoric to enhance the impact of your message and persuade your audience to take action or change their attitudes. Use words and phrases that evoke emotions, convey urgency, or inspire action, such as "imagine," "now," "must," or "change." Craft your message with precision and clarity to maximize its persuasive appeal.

9. Create a Call to Action:

- Create a clear and compelling call to action that prompts your audience to take the desired next steps after hearing your message. Whether it's signing a petition, making a donation, or changing a behavior, clearly articulate what you want your audience to do and why it's important. Use persuasive language and reasoning to motivate your audience to act on your message.

10. Engage and Involve the Audience:

- Engage your audience actively in the persuasion process by soliciting their input, asking for their opinions, or involving them in interactive activities. Encourage audience participation and dialogue to foster a sense of ownership and investment in your message and increase the likelihood of persuasion.

Encouraging Action and Response

Encouraging action and eliciting a response from your audience is a key objective of persuasive public speaking. Here are some strategies to effectively encourage action and response from your audience:

1. **Define Clear Objectives:**
   - Clearly define the desired action or response you want from your audience. Whether it's signing a petition, making a donation, changing a behavior, or simply agreeing with your viewpoint, ensure that your objectives are specific, measurable, and achievable.

2. **Highlight Benefits and Consequences:**
   - Clearly articulate the benefits of taking the desired action or the consequences of not taking action. Use persuasive language and compelling arguments to emphasize the positive outcomes or rewards that await those who respond to your message, as well as the potential risks or drawbacks of inaction.

3. **Create Urgency:**
   - Create a sense of urgency or necessity to prompt immediate action from your audience. Highlight time-sensitive opportunities, impending deadlines, or limited availability to motivate your audience to act quickly and decisively.

4. **Provide Clear Instructions:**
   - Provide clear and actionable instructions on how your audience can respond to your message. Whether it's visiting a website, making a phone call, filling out a form, or participating in a specific activity, clearly communicate the steps your audience needs to take to follow through on your call to action.

5. **Use Social Proof:**

- Use social proof to demonstrate that others have already taken the desired action and experienced positive outcomes. Share testimonials, success stories, or examples of peer behavior to show that responding to your message is a normative and desirable behavior.

6. Appeal to Emotions:

- Appeal to your audience's emotions to inspire empathy, compassion, or excitement about taking action. Use storytelling, vivid imagery, or emotional language to evoke strong emotions and motivate your audience to respond to your message with enthusiasm and conviction.

7. Offer Incentives or Rewards:

- Offer incentives or rewards to incentivize your audience to take action. Whether it's offering discounts, rewards, or exclusive benefits to those who respond to your message, provide tangible incentives that motivate your audience to act in their own best interests.

8. Address Objections and Barriers:

- Anticipate and address any objections or barriers that may prevent your audience from taking action. Provide reassurance, address concerns, or offer solutions to common obstacles to make it easier for your audience to respond to your message without hesitation.

9. Engage in Two-Way Communication:

- Foster two-way communication with your audience to encourage active participation and dialogue. Encourage questions, feedback, or contributions from your audience to create a sense of ownership and involvement in the response process.

10. Follow Up and Reinforce:

- Follow up with your audience after the presentation to reinforce your message and encourage continued action. Provide additional information, resources, or support to help your audience follow through on their response and achieve their desired outcomes.

11. Lead by Example:

- Lead by example and demonstrate your commitment to the cause or issue you're advocating for. Show that you're personally invested in the outcome and willing to take action yourself, which can inspire your audience to follow suit and respond to your message with equal enthusiasm and dedication.

12. Measure and Evaluate:
   - Measure and evaluate the effectiveness of your efforts to encourage action and response from your audience. Track key metrics, such as response rates, engagement levels, or outcomes achieved, and use this feedback to refine and improve your approach for future speaking engagements.

Evaluating Your Impact on the Audience

Evaluating your impact on the audience is essential for assessing the effectiveness of your public speaking and identifying areas for improvement. Here are some key methods for evaluating your impact on the audience:

1. Feedback Surveys:
   - Distribute feedback surveys to audience members after your presentation to gather their impressions, opinions, and suggestions for improvement. Ask questions about the clarity of your message, the effectiveness of your delivery, and the relevance of your content to gauge the audience's overall satisfaction and perception of your presentation.

2. Audience Engagement:
   - Observe the level of audience engagement and interaction during your presentation to assess how well you captured their attention and maintained their interest. Take note of audience reactions, such as laughter, nods of agreement, or applause, as indicators of engagement and receptiveness to your message.

3. Body Language and Nonverbal Cues:
   - Pay attention to audience body language and nonverbal cues to gauge their level of interest, understanding, and engagement. Look for signs of attentiveness, such as eye contact, nodding, leaning forward, or active participation, as well as signs of disengagement, such as fidgeting, checking phones, or distracted behavior.

4. Post-Presentation Discussions:

- Initiate post-presentation discussions or Q&A sessions to engage with audience members directly and gather their feedback and insights. Encourage audience members to share their thoughts, ask questions, or provide comments on your presentation, and listen attentively to their responses to gain valuable insights into their perceptions and experiences.

5. Peer Review:

- Seek feedback from peers, colleagues, or mentors who attended your presentation to gain an external perspective on your performance. Ask for honest and constructive feedback on your delivery, content, and overall effectiveness as a speaker, and use their insights to identify strengths and areas for improvement.

6. Recording and Reviewing:

- Record video or audio footage of your presentation to review your performance objectively and identify areas for improvement. Pay attention to your vocal delivery, body language, pacing, and overall presentation style, and assess how well you communicated your message and engaged with the audience.

7. Self-Reflection:

- Engage in self-reflection to evaluate your own performance and assess the impact of your presentation on the audience. Reflect on what went well, what could have been improved, and what lessons you can learn from the experience to enhance your public speaking skills and effectiveness in future presentations.

8. Assessment of Objectives:

- Evaluate the extent to which you achieved your objectives for the presentation in terms of influencing audience attitudes, beliefs, or behaviors. Assess whether you successfully communicated your key messages, persuaded your audience to take action, or achieved the desired outcomes of your presentation.

9. Comparative Analysis:

- Compare your presentation to previous speaking engagements or to presentations delivered by other speakers to benchmark your performance and identify areas of strength and weakness. Look for patterns, trends, or areas where you can improve based on comparative analysis and feedback from multiple sources.

10. Iterative Improvement:
   - Use the feedback and insights gathered from audience evaluations to iteratively improve your public speaking skills and refine your presentation techniques. Incorporate lessons learned from each speaking engagement into your practice and preparation process to continuously enhance your impact on the audience.

Chapter 11
Specialized Public Speaking Scenarios

Speaking at Conferences and Seminars

Speaking at conferences and seminars presents unique opportunities and challenges for public speakers. Here are some practical strategies for delivering effective presentations in these specialized public speaking scenarios:

1. **Know Your Audience:**
   - Research your audience demographics, interests, and expectations beforehand to tailor your presentation to their needs and interests. Understand the level of expertise and familiarity with the topic to ensure your content is relevant and engaging for attendees.

2. **Clarify Your Objectives:**
   - Define clear objectives for your presentation, such as informing, persuading, or inspiring your audience. Clarify what you want attendees to learn, understand, or take away from your presentation to guide your content and delivery.

3. **Craft Compelling Content:**
   - Develop engaging and informative content that captures the audience's attention and adds value to their conference or seminar experience. Use storytelling, case studies, statistics, and examples to illustrate key points and make your presentation memorable and impactful.

4. **Structure Your Presentation:**
   - Structure your presentation in a clear and logical manner, with a strong introduction, well-defined main points, and a compelling conclusion. Use signposts and transitions to guide the audience through your presentation and keep them engaged from start to finish.

5. **Utilize Visual Aids:**
   - Incorporate visual aids, such as slides, videos, or infographics, to enhance the clarity and impact of your presentation. Use visuals sparingly and strategically to support your key points and reinforce your message without overwhelming or distracting the audience.

6. **Engage the Audience:**

- Foster audience engagement and interaction throughout your presentation to keep attendees actively involved and invested in your message. Encourage questions, discussions, or interactive exercises that invite participation and facilitate dialogue with the audience.

7. Practice Effective Delivery:

- Practice your delivery to ensure confidence, clarity, and professionalism on stage. Rehearse your presentation multiple times, focusing on vocal delivery, body language, and pacing to maximize your impact and convey confidence to the audience.

8. Manage Time Effectively:

- Manage your time effectively to ensure that you cover all key points within the allocated timeframe. Practice pacing and timing during rehearsals to avoid rushing through content or exceeding the allotted time for your presentation.

9. Handle Q&A Sessions:

- Prepare for the Q&A session by anticipating potential questions and formulating thoughtful responses in advance. Encourage audience participation by inviting questions and facilitating constructive dialogue with attendees during the Q&A portion of your presentation.

10. Follow Up and Networking:

- Capitalize on the opportunity to network and connect with attendees after your presentation. Be approachable, friendly, and open to conversations with conference or seminar participants to build relationships, share insights, and expand your professional network.

11. Seek Feedback and Evaluate:

- Solicit feedback from conference organizers, attendees, or colleagues to assess the effectiveness of your presentation and identify areas for improvement. Reflect on your performance and evaluate what went well and what could be enhanced for future speaking engagements.

Presenting in Business Meetings

Presenting in business meetings requires a strategic approach to effectively communicate your message and achieve your objectives. Here's a practical guide for delivering successful presentations in business meetings:

1. Understand Your Audience:
   - Familiarize yourself with the attendees' roles, interests, and level of familiarity with the topic. Tailor your presentation to address their specific needs, concerns, and priorities to ensure relevance and engagement.

2. Define Clear Objectives:
   - Clarify the purpose and objectives of your presentation, whether it's to inform, persuade, or seek approval. Set specific goals for what you want to achieve by the end of the meeting to guide your content and delivery.

3. Keep it Concise and Relevant:
   - Respect the limited time available in business meetings by keeping your presentation concise and focused on the most relevant information. Stick to key points and avoid unnecessary details or tangents to ensure clarity and effectiveness.

4. Highlight Key Takeaways:
   - Emphasize the key takeaways or actionable insights that you want attendees to remember and act upon after the meeting. Use clear and concise language to communicate your main points and ensure understanding.

5. Utilize Visual Aids Sparingly:
   - Use visual aids, such as slides or charts, to support your presentation and enhance understanding. Keep visual elements simple, clear, and easy to follow, and avoid overcrowding slides with excessive text or data.

6. Engage the Audience:
   - Foster engagement and interaction by inviting questions, feedback, or input from meeting participants. Encourage dialogue and discussion

to promote collaboration and ensure that everyone feels involved and
valued.

7. Address Challenges and Solutions:

- Anticipate potential challenges or objections that may arise during
the meeting and be prepared to address them proactively. Offer
practical solutions or alternatives to overcome obstacles and
demonstrate your preparedness and problem-solving abilities.

8. Practice Effective Delivery:

- Practice your delivery to ensure confidence, clarity, and
professionalism during the meeting. Rehearse your presentation
multiple times, paying attention to vocal delivery, body language, and
pacing to convey authority and credibility.

9. Manage Time Effectively:

- Respect the agenda and time constraints of the meeting by
managing your time effectively. Stick to the allocated time for your
presentation and leave ample time for questions and discussion to
ensure a productive and efficient meeting.

10. Follow Up and Action Items:

- Summarize key points and action items at the end of your
presentation to reinforce understanding and facilitate follow-up.
Clearly articulate next steps, responsibilities, and deadlines to ensure
accountability and progress after the meeting.

11. Seek Feedback and Evaluate:

- Solicit feedback from meeting participants or colleagues to assess
the effectiveness of your presentation and identify areas for
improvement. Reflect on your performance and evaluate what went
well and what could be enhanced for future business meetings.

Toasts and Special Occasion Speeches

Delivering toasts and special occasion speeches can be memorable and
meaningful experiences for both the speaker and the audience. Here's

a practical guide to help you deliver effective speeches on special occasions:

1. Understand the Occasion:
   - Familiarize yourself with the purpose and significance of the event or occasion you're speaking at. Consider the tone, theme, and atmosphere of the gathering to tailor your speech accordingly.

2. Know Your Audience:
   - Consider the demographics, relationships, and preferences of the attendees when crafting your speech. Tailor your content and tone to resonate with the audience and evoke the appropriate emotions for the occasion.

3. Plan Your Message:
   - Define the key message or theme you want to convey in your speech. Whether it's celebrating achievements, expressing gratitude, or honoring individuals, ensure that your message aligns with the purpose and sentiment of the occasion.

4. Structure Your Speech:
   - Structure your speech in a clear and organized manner, with a well-defined introduction, body, and conclusion. Start with a captivating opening to grab the audience's attention, followed by the main content of your speech, and end with a memorable closing that reinforces your message.

5. Personalize Your Content:
   - Incorporate personal anecdotes, stories, or experiences to add authenticity and relatability to your speech. Share heartfelt sentiments, fond memories, or meaningful reflections that resonate with the audience and make your speech more engaging and memorable.

6. Keep it Concise:
   - Keep your speech concise and focused on the most relevant and impactful points. Avoid rambling or going off on tangents, and stick to the main message to maintain the audience's attention and ensure clarity and effectiveness.

7. Practice Delivery:

- Practice your speech delivery multiple times to ensure confidence, fluency, and authenticity. Pay attention to your vocal tone, pace, and body language to convey sincerity and emotion while speaking.

8. Use Humor Appropriately:

- Incorporate humor or lighthearted anecdotes to add levity and entertainment to your speech, but be mindful of the occasion and audience sensitivities. Use humor tastefully and appropriately to enhance engagement and connection with the audience.

9. Express Gratitude and Appreciation:

- Express genuine gratitude and appreciation to the individuals or groups being honored or celebrated. Acknowledge their contributions, achievements, or milestones with sincerity and warmth, and convey your heartfelt appreciation for their presence and participation in the event.

10. Engage the Audience:

- Engage the audience actively by inviting participation, interaction, or response during your speech. Encourage laughter, applause, or reflection to create a sense of camaraderie and connection among attendees and enhance the overall experience of the occasion.

11. Maintain Poise and Confidence:

- Maintain poise and confidence while delivering your speech, regardless of any nerves or emotions you may be feeling. Stand tall, make eye contact with the audience, and speak with conviction and sincerity to command attention and respect as a speaker.

12. End with a Toast or Blessing:

- Conclude your speech with a heartfelt toast, blessing, or well-wishes that encapsulate the spirit and significance of the occasion. Raise a glass or offer a symbolic gesture of celebration to mark the culmination of your speech and bring the audience together in unity and camaraderie.

Public Speaking in Educational Settings

Public speaking in educational settings presents unique challenges and opportunities for speakers to engage with students, educators, and academic audiences. Here's a practical guide for delivering effective presentations in educational settings:

1. **Know Your Audience:**
   - Understand the demographics, interests, and academic backgrounds of the audience, whether they are students, teachers, administrators, or parents. Tailor your content and delivery style to resonate with the educational context and the needs of the audience.

2. **Define Clear Objectives:**
   - Clarify the purpose and objectives of your presentation, whether it's to educate, inform, inspire, or provoke critical thinking. Align your content and messaging with the learning outcomes and expectations of the educational setting to maximize relevance and impact.

3. **Adapt Content to Grade Level:**
   - Adapt your content and language to the appropriate grade level or academic level of the audience. Use terminology, examples, and concepts that are age-appropriate and accessible to ensure understanding and engagement across diverse student populations.

4. **Use Visual Aids Effectively:**
   - Incorporate visual aids, such as slides, diagrams, or multimedia presentations, to enhance comprehension and retention of key concepts. Use visuals strategically to illustrate complex ideas, stimulate interest, and reinforce learning objectives in an engaging and interactive manner.

5. **Foster Active Learning:**
   - Foster active learning and participation by incorporating interactive elements, such as group discussions, hands-on activities, or collaborative exercises, into your presentation. Encourage students to ask questions, share their perspectives, and actively engage with the content to deepen their understanding and retention.

6. Provide Real-World Relevance:

- Relate your presentation content to real-world examples, applications, or current events to make it relevant and meaningful to students' lives and experiences. Connect academic concepts to practical implications and real-life scenarios to demonstrate their significance and relevance beyond the classroom.

7. Encourage Critical Thinking:

- Stimulate critical thinking and inquiry by posing thought-provoking questions, challenging assumptions, and encouraging students to analyze, evaluate, and synthesize information. Create opportunities for students to engage in reflective dialogue and problem-solving to develop higher-order thinking skills and intellectual curiosity.

8. Create a Positive Learning Environment:

- Create a supportive and inclusive learning environment that encourages participation, collaboration, and respect among students and educators. Foster a sense of belonging and community where diverse perspectives are valued and students feel empowered to express themselves and engage in open dialogue.

9. Demonstrate Passion and Enthusiasm:

- Demonstrate passion and enthusiasm for your subject matter to inspire curiosity and excitement among students. Use storytelling, humor, or personal anecdotes to convey your enthusiasm and make the content come alive for students, fostering a love of learning and intellectual engagement.

10. Assess Understanding and Feedback:

- Assess student understanding and learning progress throughout your presentation through formative assessments, quizzes, or informal checks for understanding. Solicit feedback from students and educators to gauge their comprehension, address any misconceptions, and adapt your approach as needed to support student learning.

11. Promote Lifelong Learning Skills:

- Promote the development of lifelong learning skills, such as critical thinking, communication, collaboration, and information literacy, through your presentation. Emphasize the value of these skills in academic success, personal growth, and future career opportunities to empower students as self-directed learners and critical thinkers.

12. Follow Up and Continued Engagement:

- Follow up with students and educators after your presentation to reinforce learning objectives, address lingering questions, and encourage continued engagement with the content. Provide resources, reading materials, or opportunities for further exploration to support ongoing learning and academic growth beyond the presentation.

Political Speeches and Public Addresses

Delivering political speeches and public addresses requires careful planning, persuasive communication, and effective delivery to engage and influence audiences. Here's a practical guide for delivering impactful political speeches and public addresses:

1. Know Your Audience:

- Understand the demographics, interests, and concerns of your audience, whether they are constituents, supporters, or members of the general public. Tailor your message and delivery to resonate with the values, priorities, and aspirations of the audience.

2. Define Clear Objectives:

- Clarify the purpose and objectives of your speech, whether it's to rally support, articulate policy positions, inspire action, or mobilize voters. Set specific goals for what you want to achieve by the end of your address to guide your content and delivery.

3. Craft Compelling Content:

- Develop a strong and persuasive message that resonates with your audience and reinforces your political platform or agenda. Use storytelling, evidence, and rhetorical techniques to convey your message with clarity, credibility, and emotional resonance.

4. Structure Your Speech:

- Structure your speech in a clear and organized manner, with a powerful introduction, well-defined main points, and a memorable conclusion. Use signposts and transitions to guide the audience through your speech and reinforce key messages effectively.

5. Use Powerful Language:
   - Use powerful and persuasive language to capture the audience's attention and convey your message with impact. Use rhetorical devices, such as repetition, parallelism, and emotive language, to enhance the persuasiveness and memorability of your speech.

6. Address Key Issues:
   - Address key issues and concerns that are relevant to your audience and demonstrate your understanding of their needs and priorities. Articulate your positions on important policy matters, offer solutions to pressing challenges, and inspire confidence in your ability to lead and effect change.

7. Engage the Audience:
   - Foster engagement and interaction by connecting with the audience emotionally and intellectually. Use anecdotes, humor, or personal experiences to establish rapport and build credibility with the audience, and encourage applause, cheers, or chants to energize and mobilize supporters.

8. Handle Opposition and Criticism:
   - Anticipate potential opposition or criticism and be prepared to address it confidently and diplomatically. Acknowledge dissenting viewpoints respectfully, offer counterarguments or rebuttals as needed, and demonstrate your ability to engage in constructive dialogue and debate.

9. Practice Effective Delivery:
   - Practice your delivery to ensure confidence, clarity, and charisma on stage. Rehearse your speech multiple times, paying attention to vocal delivery, body language, and pacing to command attention and convey authenticity as a speaker.

10. Harness the Power of Technology:
   - Utilize technology, such as teleprompters, microphones, and audiovisual equipment, to enhance the impact and reach of your

speech. Leverage social media platforms, live streaming, and digital communication tools to amplify your message and engage with a wider audience online.

11. Address the Needs of Your Constituents:
   - Demonstrate your commitment to serving the needs and interests of your constituents by addressing their concerns and advocating for policies that benefit the community. Showcase your track record of accomplishments, initiatives, and public service efforts to build trust and confidence in your leadership.

12. Follow Up and Continued Engagement:
   - Follow up with your audience after your speech to reinforce your message, address lingering questions, and encourage continued engagement and support. Provide opportunities for constituents to connect with your campaign or political organization, volunteer their time, or contribute to your cause.

Chapter 12
Public Speaking Ethics

The Responsibility of a Public Speaker

The responsibility of a public speaker encompasses a range of ethical considerations that govern their conduct, communication, and impact on audiences. Here's a practical guide outlining the key aspects of a public speaker's responsibility:

1. **Authenticity and Integrity:**
   - A public speaker has a responsibility to be authentic and genuine in their communication, presenting themselves and their message with honesty and transparency. Uphold high standards of integrity, avoiding deception, manipulation, or misrepresentation of facts to maintain credibility and trustworthiness with the audience.

2. **Respect for Diversity:**
   - Respect the diversity of perspectives, experiences, and backgrounds within the audience, acknowledging and valuing differences in opinions, beliefs, and identities. Avoid language or behavior that is discriminatory, prejudiced, or offensive, and strive to create an inclusive and respectful environment for all audience members.

3. **Accuracy and Truthfulness:**
   - Ensure the accuracy and truthfulness of the information presented in your speech, citing credible sources and verifying facts to avoid spreading misinformation or falsehoods. Take responsibility for the content of your speech, acknowledging uncertainties or limitations in your knowledge and expertise.

4. **Consideration of Consequences:**
   - Consider the potential consequences and impact of your words and actions on the audience, society, and individuals affected by your message. Exercise caution and sensitivity when discussing sensitive topics or controversial issues, recognizing the potential for harm or offense to vulnerable populations.

5. **Empathy and Compassion:**
   - Demonstrate empathy and compassion towards the audience, recognizing their emotions, concerns, and needs. Strive to connect with audience members on a human level, acknowledging their

experiences and demonstrating understanding and empathy for their perspectives and struggles.

6. Accountability and Responsibility:

- Accept accountability and responsibility for the consequences of your speech, recognizing the influence and power that comes with being a public speaker. Take ownership of any mistakes, errors, or misjudgments in your communication, and be willing to apologize, correct, or clarify misunderstandings as needed.

7. Ethical Use of Influence:

- Use your influence as a public speaker responsibly and ethically, avoiding undue influence or manipulation of the audience for personal gain or advantage. Respect the autonomy and agency of audience members, empowering them to make informed decisions based on their own values and judgment.

8. Promotion of Public Good:

- Use your platform as a public speaker to promote the public good and advance positive social change, advocating for justice, equality, and human rights. Address pressing societal issues, raise awareness of important causes, and inspire action and engagement among audience members to contribute to positive change in their communities and beyond.

9. Continuous Learning and Improvement:

- Commit to continuous learning and improvement as a public speaker, staying informed about ethical principles, best practices, and emerging issues in public speaking. Seek feedback, reflect on your performance, and engage in ongoing professional development to enhance your effectiveness and ethical conduct as a speaker.

10. Lead by Example:

- Lead by example and serve as a role model for ethical communication and responsible leadership in public speaking. Demonstrate integrity, empathy, and accountability in your words and actions, inspiring others to uphold ethical standards and contribute positively to public discourse and civic life.

Honesty and Integrity in Speech

Honesty and integrity are foundational principles that guide ethical public speaking. Here's a practical guide outlining how public speakers can embody honesty and integrity in their speech:

1. Factual Accuracy:
   - Ensure that all information presented in your speech is factually accurate and supported by credible sources. Take the time to verify the accuracy of statistics, data, and claims before including them in your presentation. Avoid spreading misinformation or unsubstantiated rumors that could mislead or deceive your audience.

2. Transparency:
   - Be transparent about your intentions, affiliations, and biases when delivering a speech. Disclose any potential conflicts of interest or vested interests that may influence your perspective or presentation. Transparency builds trust with your audience and demonstrates a commitment to ethical communication.

3. Avoiding Deception:
   - Avoid deceptive or manipulative tactics in your speech, such as exaggeration, omission of key information, or misleading framing of facts. Present information in a balanced and honest manner, acknowledging complexities and nuances, even if they may challenge your argument or viewpoint.

4. Citing Sources:
   - Give credit to the original sources of information, ideas, or quotations that you incorporate into your speech. Properly cite academic research, expert opinions, and other external sources to acknowledge the contributions of others and uphold academic integrity.

5. Authenticity:
   - Be authentic and genuine in your communication, expressing your true beliefs, values, and convictions. Avoid pandering to the audience or adopting a persona that is inconsistent with your true self.

Authenticity builds rapport and credibility with your audience, fostering genuine connection and trust.

6. Accountability:

- Take responsibility for the accuracy and impact of your speech. If you make a mistake or inadvertently provide incorrect information, acknowledge it openly and correct the record. Demonstrate accountability for your words and actions, even when it requires admitting fault or making amends.

7. Respect for Diverse Perspectives:

- Respect diverse perspectives and viewpoints within your audience, even if they differ from your own. Avoid dismissing or denigrating alternative opinions, and engage in constructive dialogue that promotes mutual understanding and respect. Embrace intellectual humility and openness to learning from others.

8. Ethical Argumentation:

- Present arguments and persuasion techniques ethically, without resorting to fallacious reasoning or manipulative tactics. Use logical reasoning, evidence-based arguments, and ethical appeals to persuade your audience, rather than relying on emotional manipulation or rhetorical tricks.

9. Consistency:

- Ensure consistency between your words and actions, both within your speech and in your broader public persona. Align your speech with your personal values and ethical principles, and strive to maintain integrity and coherence in all aspects of your public communication.

10. Continuous Improvement:

- Commit to ongoing self-reflection and professional development to strengthen your ethical standards and communication skills as a public speaker. Seek feedback from trusted colleagues or mentors, reflect on ethical dilemmas you encounter, and actively seek opportunities to learn and grow in your practice.

Respecting Diversity and Inclusivity

Respecting diversity and inclusivity is essential for public speakers to create an environment where all audience members feel valued, heard, and respected. Here's a practical guide on how public speakers can uphold these principles:

1. Acknowledge Diversity:
   - Recognize and acknowledge the diversity of your audience, including differences in culture, ethnicity, gender, age, religion, socioeconomic status, and perspective. Embrace the richness of diversity as a strength and opportunity for learning and understanding.

2. Cultivate Inclusive Language:
   - Use language that is inclusive and respectful of all individuals, avoiding stereotypes, discriminatory language, or derogatory terms. Choose words and phrases that reflect sensitivity to diverse identities and experiences, and strive to create an inclusive atmosphere where everyone feels welcome and valued.

3. Respect Pronouns and Identities:
   - Respect individuals' gender identities and preferred pronouns by using the correct pronouns and terminology as indicated by each individual. Avoid making assumptions about gender identity or using gendered language that may exclude or misgender individuals.

4. Listen Actively:
   - Practice active listening and empathy to understand the perspectives and experiences of individuals from diverse backgrounds. Encourage open dialogue and feedback, and demonstrate genuine interest and respect for differing viewpoints and lived experiences.

5. Include Diverse Voices:
   - Include diverse voices and perspectives in your speech by referencing a range of sources, experts, and viewpoints. Amplify the voices of marginalized or underrepresented groups, and ensure that a variety of perspectives are represented in your content and examples.

6. Address Intersectionality:
   - Recognize the intersecting identities and experiences that shape individuals' lives, such as race, gender, sexuality, disability, and class.

Acknowledge the complex and interconnected nature of oppression and privilege, and strive to address systemic inequalities and injustices in your speech.

7. Create a Safe Space:

- Foster a safe and inclusive space for dialogue and expression where individuals feel comfortable sharing their thoughts, experiences, and concerns. Set ground rules for respectful communication, and intervene promptly to address any instances of discrimination, harassment, or disrespect.

8. Promote Accessibility:

- Ensure that your speech is accessible to individuals with disabilities by providing accommodations, such as sign language interpretation, captioning, or accessible materials. Consider the needs of individuals with visual, auditory, cognitive, or mobility impairments, and make adjustments to facilitate their participation and engagement.

9. Challenge Bias and Stereotypes:

- Challenge bias, stereotypes, and prejudice in your speech by confronting discriminatory attitudes and promoting empathy, understanding, and solidarity. Use your platform to challenge harmful narratives and promote social justice, equality, and inclusion for all individuals.

10. Lead by Example:

- Lead by example and model inclusive behavior and attitudes in your speech and actions. Demonstrate respect, empathy, and openness to diversity in your interactions with others, and advocate for inclusive practices and policies within your organization or community.

11. Seek Feedback and Learn:

- Seek feedback from diverse perspectives on your speech and communication practices, and be open to learning and growth. Actively seek out opportunities to expand your understanding of diversity and inclusion, and commit to ongoing self-education and awareness-raising.

Handling Sensitive Topics Ethically

Handling sensitive topics ethically is crucial for public speakers to navigate potentially challenging or controversial subjects in a responsible and respectful manner. Here's a practical guide on how to address sensitive topics ethically:

1. Understand the Sensitivity:
- Take time to understand the sensitivity and potential impact of the topic you're addressing. Recognize that certain subjects may evoke strong emotions, trigger trauma, or perpetuate harm if not handled with care and sensitivity.

2. Research Thoroughly:
- Conduct thorough research on the topic to ensure you have a comprehensive understanding of its complexities, historical context, and diverse perspectives. Consider consulting experts, scholars, or individuals with lived experience to gain insights and perspectives that inform your approach.

3. Consider Audience Needs:
- Consider the needs and sensitivities of your audience when addressing sensitive topics. Tailor your messaging and delivery to be respectful, empathetic, and culturally appropriate, taking into account the diversity of backgrounds, beliefs, and experiences within your audience.

4. Frame the Discussion Responsibly:
- Frame the discussion of sensitive topics responsibly, focusing on fostering understanding, empathy, and constructive dialogue rather than sensationalism, polarization, or conflict. Use language that is respectful, inclusive, and non-inflammatory to create a safe and respectful environment for discussion.

5. Acknowledge Different Perspectives:
- Acknowledge and validate different perspectives and experiences related to the sensitive topic, recognizing that there may be diverse viewpoints within your audience. Avoid presenting a one-sided or oversimplified narrative, and strive to represent a range of voices and perspectives in your presentation.

6. Provide Context and Background:

- Provide context and background information to help your audience understand the complexity and nuances of the sensitive topic. Offer historical, social, or cultural context that illuminates the roots and implications of the issue, helping to deepen audience understanding and empathy.

7. Empower Audience Reflection:

- Empower your audience to engage critically with the sensitive topic by encouraging reflection, inquiry, and dialogue. Pose thought-provoking questions, invite audience participation, and create opportunities for individuals to share their perspectives and experiences in a respectful and supportive environment.

8. Exercise Sensitivity and Empathy:

- Exercise sensitivity and empathy in your communication, recognizing the potential emotional impact of the topic on individuals in your audience. Demonstrate empathy, active listening, and compassion in your interactions, and be prepared to offer support or resources to those who may be affected.

9. Address Potential Harm:

- Consider the potential harm that discussing the sensitive topic may cause to individuals who have experienced trauma or marginalization related to the issue. Take steps to mitigate harm by providing trigger warnings, offering support resources, and creating a supportive and non-judgmental space for discussion.

10. Commit to Continued Learning:

- Commit to continued learning and growth in your understanding of sensitive topics and ethical communication practices. Stay informed about emerging issues, engage in ongoing self-reflection and education, and seek feedback from diverse perspectives to inform and improve your approach over time.

Balancing Persuasion with Ethical Considerations

Balancing persuasion with ethical considerations is essential for public speakers to influence audiences effectively while maintaining integrity and respect for ethical principles. Here's a practical guide on how to achieve this balance:

1. Clarify Your Intentions:

- Before crafting your speech, clarify your intentions and objectives. Determine whether your goal is solely to persuade or if it includes broader ethical considerations such as promoting understanding, fostering dialogue, or respecting diverse perspectives.

2. Align Persuasion with Ethical Principles:

- Ensure that your persuasive tactics align with ethical principles such as honesty, transparency, respect for autonomy, and fairness. Avoid using manipulative or deceptive tactics that undermine trust and integrity, and prioritize building credibility and rapport with your audience.

3. Provide Honest and Transparent Information:

- Present information honestly and transparently, providing a balanced view of the topic that acknowledges complexities and nuances. Avoid cherry-picking evidence or distorting facts to suit your argument, and be forthcoming about any potential biases or conflicts of interest.

4. Appeal to Reason and Emotion Responsibly:

- Appeal to both reason and emotion in your speech, but do so responsibly and ethically. Use logical reasoning, evidence-based arguments, and ethical appeals to persuade your audience, while avoiding manipulation or exploitation of emotional triggers for unethical ends.

5. Respect Audience Autonomy:

- Respect the autonomy of your audience by presenting information in a way that allows them to make informed decisions based on their own values, beliefs, and judgment. Avoid pressuring or coercing individuals into accepting your viewpoint, and encourage critical thinking and independent evaluation of the information presented.

6. Acknowledge Counterarguments and Diverse Perspectives:

- Acknowledge counterarguments and diverse perspectives on the topic, demonstrating intellectual honesty and respect for differing viewpoints. Addressing opposing viewpoints strengthens your credibility as a speaker and demonstrates a commitment to fairness and open dialogue.

7. Empower Audience Participation:

- Empower your audience to engage critically with your message and participate actively in the discussion. Encourage questions, feedback, and dialogue, and create opportunities for audience members to share their perspectives and experiences in a respectful and inclusive environment.

8. Appeal to Shared Values and Ethics:

- Appeal to shared values and ethical principles that resonate with your audience, fostering a sense of common ground and shared purpose. Emphasize the ethical implications and consequences of your message, highlighting how it aligns with principles of justice, compassion, integrity, or social responsibility.

9. Consider Long-Term Impact:

- Consider the long-term impact of your persuasive efforts on individuals, communities, and society as a whole. Strive to promote positive social change, empower marginalized voices, and advance ethical goals and values through your persuasive communication.

10. Reflect on Ethical Dilemmas:

- Reflect critically on ethical dilemmas that arise in your persuasive communication, seeking to balance the pursuit of your objectives with ethical considerations and potential consequences. Be open to feedback, self-examination, and ongoing learning to refine your approach and enhance ethical integrity in your speaking practices.

Chapter 13
Continuous Improvement in Public Speaking

Seeking Feedback and Constructive Criticism

Seeking feedback and constructive criticism is a vital aspect of continuous improvement in public speaking. Here's a practical guide on how to effectively solicit feedback and use it to enhance your public speaking skills:

1. **Create a Feedback-Friendly Environment:**
   - Foster an environment where feedback is welcomed and encouraged. Let your audience know that you value their input and are open to hearing their thoughts on your presentation.

2. **Specify the Type of Feedback You Seek:**
   - Be clear about the specific aspects of your speech or presentation that you would like feedback on. Whether it's your delivery, content structure, body language, or vocal tone, providing guidance helps respondents give targeted and actionable feedback.

3. **Ask the Right Questions:**
   - Pose specific questions that elicit helpful feedback. For example, ask about the clarity of your message, the effectiveness of your storytelling, or the impact of your visual aids. Open-ended questions can provide valuable insights into areas for improvement.

4. **Seek Feedback from Diverse Sources:**
   - Don't limit your feedback to just one source. Seek input from a variety of perspectives, including peers, mentors, instructors, and audience members. Different viewpoints can offer valuable insights and help you identify blind spots.

5. **Be Open-Minded and Receptive:**
   - Approach feedback with an open mind and a willingness to learn. Even if it's difficult to hear criticism, remember that it's an opportunity for growth. Listen attentively, ask clarifying questions, and resist the urge to become defensive.

6. **Actively Listen to Feedback:**
   - Practice active listening during feedback sessions. Focus on understanding the feedback provider's perspective, and resist the urge

to interrupt or explain away criticisms. Paraphrase what you've heard to ensure you understand correctly.

7. Take Notes and Reflect:
   - Take notes during feedback sessions to capture key points and suggestions for improvement. Set aside time to reflect on the feedback afterward, considering how you can apply it to enhance your public speaking skills.

8. Identify Patterns and Trends:
   - Look for patterns or recurring themes in the feedback you receive. If multiple people mention the same issue, it's likely an area that warrants attention. Identifying trends can help you prioritize areas for improvement.

9. Set SMART Goals:
   - Use the feedback you receive to set specific, measurable, achievable, relevant, and time-bound (SMART) goals for your public speaking development. For example, aim to reduce filler words by 50% in your next presentation or improve vocal projection by a certain decibel level.

10. Implement Actionable Changes:
   - Translate feedback into actionable changes in your public speaking practice. Experiment with new techniques, adjust your delivery style, or revise your content based on the insights you've gained. Monitor your progress and adjust your approach as needed.

11. Follow Up and Express Gratitude:
   - Follow up with those who provided feedback to express your gratitude for their insights and to share how you've implemented their suggestions. Showing appreciation for feedback encourages ongoing engagement and fosters a culture of mutual support and learning.

12. Seek Ongoing Feedback:
   - Make feedback an ongoing part of your public speaking journey. Regularly solicit feedback after presentations, workshops, or practice sessions, and use it to continually refine and enhance your skills over time.

Learning from Successful Speakers

Learning from successful speakers is an invaluable strategy for continuous improvement in public speaking. Here's a practical guide on how to effectively glean insights from accomplished speakers:

1. Study Diverse Speakers:
   - Expand your horizons by studying a diverse range of successful speakers from various backgrounds, industries, and speaking styles. Examine their techniques, delivery, and presentation content to gain a comprehensive understanding of effective public speaking.

2. Analyze Speeches Critically:
   - Watch speeches or presentations by successful speakers with a critical eye. Pay attention to their storytelling techniques, vocal delivery, body language, use of visual aids, and audience engagement strategies. Analyze what makes their speeches impactful and memorable.

3. Identify Key Strengths:
   - Identify the key strengths of successful speakers that resonate with you. Whether it's their charisma, authenticity, clarity of message, or ability to connect with the audience, pinpoint the qualities you admire and aspire to incorporate into your own speaking style.

4. Observe Delivery Techniques:
   - Observe the delivery techniques employed by successful speakers, such as their pacing, tone of voice, emphasis, and gestures. Take note of how they modulate their voice to convey emotion, maintain audience engagement, and command attention throughout their presentation.

5. Study Content Structure:
   - Study the structure of successful speeches to understand how they organize their content for maximum impact. Analyze their introduction, body, and conclusion, as well as the flow of ideas and

transitions between key points. Consider how they use storytelling, anecdotes, or evidence to support their message.

6. Examine Visual Aids and Props:
   - Pay attention to how successful speakers use visual aids, props, or multimedia elements to enhance their presentations. Assess the effectiveness of their slides, images, videos, or props in reinforcing key points and engaging the audience visually.

7. Learn from Audience Interaction:
   - Take note of how successful speakers interact with their audience during Q&A sessions or interactive segments. Observe their listening skills, responsiveness to audience questions, and ability to handle unexpected challenges or objections with grace and confidence.

8. Seek Insights from Interviews or Biographies:
   - Seek out interviews, articles, or biographies of successful speakers to gain insights into their journey, mindset, and approach to public speaking. Learn from their experiences, setbacks, and lessons learned along the way, and apply them to your own speaking practice.

9. Attend Workshops or Seminars:
   - Attend workshops, seminars, or live events featuring successful speakers to learn directly from their expertise. Take advantage of opportunities to ask questions, participate in discussions, and engage with other attendees to deepen your understanding and refine your skills.

10. Practice Emulation and Adaptation:
   - Practice emulating aspects of successful speakers' techniques in your own presentations, adapting them to suit your unique style, personality, and audience. Experiment with incorporating new techniques gradually, and assess their effectiveness through feedback and self-reflection.

11. Reflect and Iterate:
   - Reflect on your observations and insights from studying successful speakers, and use them to inform your ongoing practice and refinement. Continually iterate on your approach, integrating lessons

learned and striving for continual improvement in your public speaking
journey.

Keeping Abreast of Communication Trends

Keeping abreast of communication trends is essential for continuous
improvement in public speaking. Here's a practical guide on how to stay
updated with the latest trends in communication:

1. **Follow Industry Publications and Websites:**
   - Stay informed about communication trends by regularly reading
industry publications, blogs, and websites focused on public speaking,
presentation skills, and communication techniques. Subscribe to
newsletters or RSS feeds to receive updates directly to your inbox.

2. **Attend Conferences and Workshops:**
   - Attend conferences, workshops, and seminars on public speaking,
communication, and related fields to learn about emerging trends, best
practices, and innovative techniques from industry experts and thought
leaders. Take advantage of networking opportunities to connect with
other professionals and exchange ideas.

3. **Join Professional Associations:**
   - Join professional associations or organizations dedicated to public
speaking. Participate in meetings, webinars, and online forums to stay
informed about current trends and developments in the field.

4. **Engage on Social Media:**
   - Follow influential speakers, trainers, and communication experts on
social media platforms. Join relevant groups or communities where
professionals share insights, resources, and discussions about public
speaking and communication trends.

5. **Take Online Courses and Webinars:**
   - Enroll in online courses, webinars, or virtual workshops focused on
public speaking and presentation skills. Many platforms offer courses
taught by industry experts, covering topics ranging from storytelling
and audience engagement to multimedia presentation techniques.

6. Read Books and Publications:

- Read books, whitepapers, and academic journals on communication theory, persuasion, and public speaking. Explore titles by renowned authors in the field, and stay informed about new research findings and theoretical frameworks that can inform your practice.

7. Follow Thought Leaders and Influencers:

- Identify thought leaders, influencers, and public speakers whose work resonates with you, and follow their blogs, podcasts, and social media channels. Pay attention to their insights, observations, and predictions about communication trends and future directions in public speaking.

8. Experiment with New Technologies:

- Stay updated with advancements in technology that can enhance public speaking and presentation delivery. Experiment with new tools, software, and platforms for creating interactive presentations, incorporating multimedia elements, or engaging with virtual audiences.

9. Attend Webinars and Virtual Events:

- Participate in webinars, virtual summits, and online events focused on communication and public speaking trends. Take advantage of virtual platforms to access presentations, panel discussions, and live demonstrations from experts around the world.

10. Seek Feedback and Adaptation:

- Continuously seek feedback from peers, mentors, and audience members about your speaking style, content, and delivery. Be receptive to constructive criticism and adapt your approach to incorporate feedback and align with evolving communication trends.

11. Experiment and Innovate:

- Embrace a mindset of experimentation and innovation in your public speaking practice. Be willing to try new techniques, formats, or presentation styles, and evaluate their effectiveness based on audience feedback and engagement metrics.

Joining Public Speaking Groups and Clubs

Joining public speaking groups and clubs is an excellent way to facilitate continuous improvement in public speaking skills. Here's a practical guide on how to make the most of your participation in such groups:

1. Research Local Clubs:
   - Start by researching public speaking groups and clubs in your local area. Look for chapters of organizations where you can find structured programs and supportive communities focused on improving public speaking skills.

2. Attend Meetings:
   - Attend meetings of different public speaking groups to get a sense of their culture, structure, and format. Many clubs allow guests to attend meetings for free or for a nominal fee. Take advantage of this opportunity to observe and assess whether the club aligns with your goals and preferences.

3. Join a Club:
   - Once you've identified a club that resonates with you, consider joining as a member. Membership typically involves paying dues and committing to regular participation in club activities. Look for clubs that offer a supportive and inclusive environment conducive to learning and growth.

4. Participate Actively:
   - Actively participate in club meetings, workshops, and activities to maximize your learning experience. Volunteer for speaking roles such as prepared speeches, impromptu speaking, or speech evaluations to practice and receive feedback on your speaking skills.

5. Take on Leadership Roles:
   - Take on leadership roles within the club to develop valuable leadership skills while also contributing to the club's success. Positions such as club officer, mentor, or event organizer provide opportunities for personal growth and development beyond public speaking.

6. Practice, Practice, Practice:

- Take advantage of every opportunity to practice public speaking within the club setting. Use prepared speech assignments to work on specific aspects of your speaking skills, such as speech organization, delivery techniques, or storytelling.

7. Receive Constructive Feedback:

- Embrace feedback as a valuable tool for improvement. Actively seek feedback from club members and evaluators after each speech or presentation, and use their insights to identify areas for growth and refinement.

8. Offer Feedback to Others:

- Participate in speech evaluations and offer constructive feedback to fellow club members. Providing feedback not only helps others improve their speaking skills but also enhances your ability to analyze and articulate effective speaking techniques.

9. Attend Workshops and Training Sessions:

- Take advantage of workshops, training sessions, and educational programs offered by the club or organization. These sessions often cover a wide range of topics related to public speaking, presentation skills, leadership, and personal development.

10. Network and Build Relationships:

- Use club meetings and events as opportunities to network and build relationships with other public speakers and professionals. Exchange ideas, share experiences, and collaborate on projects with like-minded individuals who share your passion for public speaking.

11. Set Goals and Track Progress:

- Set specific goals for your public speaking development and track your progress over time. Whether it's completing a certain number of speeches, achieving a particular competency level, or conquering a fear of public speaking, having clear goals can help keep you motivated and focused on improvement.

12. Celebrate Achievements:

- Celebrate your achievements and milestones along the way. Recognize and acknowledge your progress, no matter how small, and use each success as motivation to continue pushing yourself to new heights in your public speaking journey.

Developing a Personalized Growth Plan

Developing a personalized growth plan is essential for continuous improvement in public speaking. Here's a practical guide on how to create a plan tailored to your specific goals and needs:

1. **Set Clear Objectives:**
   - Start by defining your objectives and what you hope to achieve through your public speaking journey. Whether it's overcoming stage fright, improving vocal delivery, or mastering storytelling techniques, having clear goals will guide your growth plan.

2. **Assess Your Current Skills:**
   - Conduct a self-assessment to identify your current strengths and areas for improvement in public speaking. Reflect on past speaking experiences, feedback received, and areas where you feel confident versus areas where you struggle.

3. **Identify Areas for Development:**
   - Based on your self-assessment, identify specific areas of public speaking that you want to develop or refine. These may include content creation, vocal delivery, body language, audience engagement, or overcoming nerves.

4. **Research Resources and Tools:**
   - Research resources, tools, and learning opportunities that can help you address the areas you've identified for development. Consider books, online courses, workshops, podcasts, or coaching programs that align with your objectives.

5. **Create a Timeline:**
   - Establish a timeline for your growth plan, setting realistic deadlines and milestones for achieving your objectives. Break down larger goals

into smaller, manageable tasks that you can work on incrementally over time.

6. Prioritize Learning Activities:
   - Prioritize learning activities based on their relevance to your goals and the areas you've identified for development. Allocate time each week or month for focused practice, study, and reflection.

7. Practice Regularly:
   - Dedicate time to regular practice sessions to hone your public speaking skills. Practice delivering speeches, presentations, or pitches in front of a mirror, recording yourself for self-assessment, or seeking opportunities to speak in front of small groups.

8. Seek Feedback and Evaluation:
   - Actively seek feedback and evaluation from peers, mentors, or public speaking groups to gain insights into your strengths and areas for improvement. Use this feedback to adjust your approach and refine your skills.

9. Attend Workshops and Training:
   - Take advantage of workshops, training sessions, and educational programs that offer opportunities to learn new techniques and strategies for effective public speaking. Look for topics that align with your growth objectives and attend sessions led by experts in the field.

10. Reflect and Adapt:
   - Regularly reflect on your progress and adjust your growth plan as needed. Celebrate achievements, learn from setbacks, and adapt your approach based on what's working well and what needs improvement.

11. Stay Inspired and Motivated:
   - Stay inspired and motivated by seeking inspiration from successful speakers, setting incremental goals, and celebrating progress along the way. Surround yourself with supportive peers and mentors who encourage your growth and provide motivation when needed.

12. Track Your Progress:

- Keep track of your progress towards your goals by maintaining a journal, checklist, or progress tracker. Document achievements, milestones, and lessons learned to stay accountable and measure your growth over time.

Chapter 14
Leveraging Technology in Public Speaking

Online Public Speaking and Webinars

Leveraging technology for online public speaking and webinars is becoming increasingly prevalent in today's digital age. Here's a practical guide on how to effectively utilize technology for these purposes:

1. Choose the Right Platform:
- Select a reliable and user-friendly platform for hosting online public speaking engagements and webinars. Consider factors such as ease of use, features, audience size limitations, and compatibility with your needs.

2. Set Up Your Environment:
- Create a professional and distraction-free environment for online presentations. Choose a quiet, well-lit space with minimal background noise and distractions. Ensure that your background is tidy and appropriate for the context of your presentation.

3. Invest in Quality Equipment:
- Invest in quality audiovisual equipment to ensure clear communication during online public speaking engagements. Use a high-quality microphone, webcam, and lighting setup to enhance audio and video quality. Consider using a headset with a microphone to minimize background noise.

4. Test Technology in Advance:
- Conduct a thorough technology test before your online presentation or webinar to ensure everything is working properly. Test your audio, video, screen sharing, and presentation slides to identify and address any technical issues beforehand.

5. Engage Your Audience:
- Keep your audience engaged throughout the online presentation by incorporating interactive elements such as polls, Q&A sessions, chat features, and audience participation activities. Encourage attendees to ask questions and provide feedback to foster interaction and dialogue.

6. Adapt Content for Online Delivery:

- Adapt your content and delivery style for online presentations to suit the medium. Keep slides concise and visually appealing, use engaging visuals to support key points, and avoid information overload. Speak clearly and at a moderate pace to ensure comprehension.

7. Practice Effective Delivery Techniques:
- Practice effective delivery techniques for online public speaking, including maintaining eye contact with the camera, using gestures and facial expressions to convey emotion, and modulating your voice for emphasis. Practice speaking naturally and confidently to establish rapport with your audience.

8. Manage Time Effectively:
- Manage your time effectively during online presentations and webinars to ensure that you cover all planned content within the allotted time. Create a detailed agenda or outline and stick to it to maintain a smooth flow and avoid running over time.

9. Provide Value-Added Content:
- Provide value-added content that addresses the needs and interests of your audience. Offer practical tips, insights, case studies, or actionable strategies that attendees can apply in their personal or professional lives. Tailor your content to the specific interests and preferences of your audience.

10. Promote Your Online Events:
- Promote your online public speaking engagements and webinars through various channels to attract attendees. Use social media, email marketing, website announcements, and online event platforms to spread the word and generate interest in your presentation.

11. Gather Feedback and Evaluate:
- Gather feedback from attendees after your online events to evaluate their effectiveness and identify areas for improvement. Use surveys, polls, or post-event discussions to collect feedback on content, delivery, technology, and overall experience.

12. Continuously Improve:

- Continuously evaluate and improve your online public speaking skills based on feedback, self-reflection, and learning opportunities. Stay updated on emerging trends, best practices, and new technologies in online communication to remain effective and relevant in your digital presentations.

Using Social Media to Enhance Your Presence

Using social media to enhance your presence is a valuable strategy for public speakers seeking to expand their reach and engage with their audience. Here's a practical guide on how to effectively leverage social media for public speaking:

1. **Choose the Right Platforms:**
   - Identify the social media platforms that align with your target audience and communication objectives. Focus on platforms where your audience is most active and engaged.

2. **Optimize Your Profiles:**
   - Optimize your social media profiles to reflect your expertise, personality, and speaking topics. Use a professional profile photo, write a compelling bio that highlights your experience and credentials, and include relevant keywords and hashtags to make your profile more discoverable.

3. **Share Valuable Content:**
   - Share valuable and relevant content that resonates with your audience. This could include tips, insights, articles, videos, infographics, or behind-the-scenes glimpses of your speaking engagements. Create original content that showcases your expertise and provides value to your followers.

4. **Engage with Your Audience:**
   - Foster engagement with your audience by responding to comments, messages, and mentions promptly. Encourage discussions, ask questions, and seek feedback to create a dialogue with your followers. Engage authentically and genuinely to build rapport and strengthen relationships.

5. Promote Your Speaking Engagements:

- Use social media to promote your speaking engagements, workshops, webinars, or events. Create event pages, share event details, and post updates leading up to the event to generate excitement and encourage attendance. Share photos, testimonials, or highlights from past speaking engagements to showcase your expertise and credibility.

6. Share Behind-the-Scenes Content:

- Share behind-the-scenes content to give your audience a glimpse into your life as a speaker. This could include photos or videos of your preparation process, rehearsals, travel experiences, or interactions with audience members. Humanize your brand and make personal connections with your followers.

7. Utilize Visuals Effectively:

- Use visual content such as images, graphics, videos, and infographics to enhance the visibility and impact of your social media posts. Visuals are more engaging and shareable than text-only posts and can help capture your audience's attention in crowded social media feeds.

8. Establish Thought Leadership:

- Position yourself as a thought leader in your niche by sharing valuable insights, thought-provoking ideas, and thought leadership content on social media. Share your expertise, offer solutions to common challenges, and contribute to relevant discussions within your industry or field of expertise.

9. Network with Industry Professionals:

- Use social media to network with other public speakers, industry professionals, event organizers, and influencers in your field. Connect with like-minded individuals, join relevant groups or communities, and participate in discussions to expand your network and build mutually beneficial relationships.

10. Create Consistent Branding:

- Maintain consistent branding across your social media profiles to reinforce your identity as a public speaker. Use consistent imagery, colors, fonts, and messaging to create a cohesive brand presence that reflects your personality and speaking style.

11. **Track Performance and Analytics:**
   - Monitor your social media performance and analytics to track the effectiveness of your efforts. Use built-in analytics tools or third-party analytics platforms to measure key metrics such as engagement, reach, followers growth, and website traffic. Use these insights to refine your strategy and optimize your social media presence over time.

12. **Stay Authentic and Genuine:**
   - Above all, stay authentic and genuine in your interactions on social media. Be yourself, share your story, and express your passion for public speaking authentically. Build trust with your audience by being transparent, honest, and true to your values as a speaker.

Podcasting and Audio-Based Public Speaking

Podcasting and audio-based public speaking present unique opportunities for reaching and engaging with audiences who prefer audio content. Here's a practical guide on how to effectively leverage podcasting and audio-based platforms for public speaking:

1. **Define Your Podcasting Goals:**
   - Start by defining clear goals for your podcasting efforts. Determine the purpose of your podcast, your target audience, and the topics you'll cover. Consider how podcasting aligns with your overall public speaking objectives and how it can complement your existing content.

2. **Choose Your Podcast Format:**
   - Choose a podcast format that suits your content and audience preferences. Common formats include solo episodes, interviews, panel discussions, storytelling, or a combination of formats. Decide on the structure, length, and frequency of your episodes based on your content and audience needs.

3. Invest in Quality Equipment:

   - Invest in quality recording equipment to ensure professional audio quality for your podcast. This includes a good microphone, headphones, audio interface, and recording software. Choose equipment that fits your budget and technical requirements while delivering clear and crisp sound.

4. Plan and Script Your Episodes:

   - Plan and script your podcast episodes in advance to ensure clarity, structure, and coherence. Outline key talking points, organize your content logically, and script any intros, outros, or transitions to maintain a smooth flow. Practice reading your script aloud to ensure natural delivery.

5. Focus on Engaging Content:

   - Create engaging and valuable content that resonates with your target audience. Provide actionable insights, practical tips, entertaining stories, or thought-provoking discussions that keep listeners engaged and coming back for more. Be authentic, relatable, and genuine in your delivery.

6. Promote Your Podcast:

   - Promote your podcast across various channels to increase visibility and attract listeners. Share episodes on social media, your website, email newsletters, and relevant online communities. Consider collaborating with other podcasters, influencers, or industry experts to expand your reach.

7. Optimize for Search and Discovery:

   - Optimize your podcast for search and discovery to improve its visibility on podcast platforms and search engines. Choose a descriptive title and relevant keywords, write compelling episode titles and descriptions, and use tags or categories to help listeners find your content.

8. Engage with Your Audience:

   - Foster engagement with your audience by encouraging feedback, questions, and listener submissions. Invite listeners to share their thoughts, stories, or questions and incorporate listener feedback into future episodes. Respond to listener inquiries, comments, and reviews to build rapport and strengthen relationships.

9. Invite Guest Speakers:
- Invite guest speakers, experts, or influencers to join you on your podcast as guests. Hosting guest interviews adds variety, credibility, and fresh perspectives to your content while expanding your network and reaching new audiences. Choose guests who align with your podcast's theme and provide valuable insights for your audience.

10. Monitor and Analyze Performance:
- Monitor the performance of your podcast using analytics tools provided by podcast hosting platforms or third-party analytics services. Track metrics such as downloads, listens, subscriber growth, listener demographics, and engagement levels. Use this data to evaluate the effectiveness of your content and make informed decisions about future episodes.

11. Stay Consistent and Reliable:
- Maintain a consistent publishing schedule and deliver episodes reliably to keep your audience engaged and coming back for more. Establish expectations for your audience regarding episode frequency and release times, and strive to meet or exceed those expectations consistently.

12. Continuously Improve and Adapt:
- Continuously seek feedback from listeners, evaluate listener engagement and satisfaction, and adapt your podcasting strategy accordingly. Experiment with new formats, topics, or promotional tactics based on audience preferences and feedback to keep your podcast fresh and relevant.

Virtual Reality and Augmented Reality in Speech Delivery

Leveraging virtual reality (VR) and augmented reality (AR) in speech delivery presents innovative opportunities to enhance engagement and immersion for both speakers and audiences. Here's a practical guide on how to effectively incorporate VR and AR into public speaking:

1. Understand VR and AR Technology:

- Familiarize yourself with the principles and capabilities of VR and AR technology. VR immerses users in a computer-generated environment, while AR overlays digital content onto the real world. Understand how these technologies can be used to enhance speech delivery and audience interaction.

2. Choose the Right Platform:

- Select a VR or AR platform that aligns with your objectives and audience preferences. Consider platforms, or mobile AR apps. Choose a platform that offers the features and functionality you need for your speech delivery.

3. Design Immersive Environments:

- Design immersive virtual environments or augmented reality overlays that enhance the delivery of your speech. Create visually appealing backgrounds, interactive elements, and 3D visuals that complement your message and engage your audience. Consider incorporating virtual stages, props, or visual effects to captivate your audience's attention.

4. Practice in VR/AR Environments:

- Practice delivering your speech in VR or AR environments to familiarize yourself with the technology and refine your presentation skills. Use VR/AR simulations to rehearse different scenarios, experiment with delivery techniques, and adjust your performance based on real-time feedback.

5. Utilize Interactive Features:

- Take advantage of interactive features and functionalities offered by VR and AR platforms to engage your audience. Incorporate interactive polls, quizzes, surveys, or games that encourage audience participation and feedback. Use gestures, hand movements, or voice commands to navigate virtual environments and interact with digital content.

6. Enhance Visual and Audio Elements:

- Enhance visual and audio elements of your speech using VR and AR technology. Incorporate high-quality visuals, 3D animations, spatial audio, and immersive soundscapes to create a multisensory experience for your audience. Use visual cues and audio cues to guide audience attention and reinforce key points.

7. Customize Content for VR/AR:

- Customize your speech content and delivery style to suit the immersive nature of VR and AR environments. Adapt your storytelling techniques, pacing, and engagement strategies to leverage the unique capabilities of these technologies. Design content that takes advantage of 3D space, depth perception, and interactivity to captivate your audience.

8. Provide Virtual Audience Interaction:

- Provide opportunities for virtual audience interaction and engagement within VR and AR environments. Allow audience members to ask questions, participate in discussions, or interact with digital content in real-time. Create virtual networking opportunities or social spaces where audience members can connect with each other and with you as the speaker.

9. Manage Technical Considerations:

- Anticipate and address technical considerations associated with VR and AR speech delivery. Ensure stable internet connection, compatible hardware and software, and sufficient technical support to troubleshoot any issues that may arise during your presentation. Practice using VR/AR equipment and familiarize yourself with platform-specific features to minimize technical disruptions.

10. Gather Feedback and Evaluate Impact:

- Gather feedback from your audience regarding their experience with VR and AR speech delivery. Solicit feedback on usability, immersion, engagement, and overall effectiveness of the technology in enhancing their understanding and retention of your message. Use audience feedback to evaluate the impact of VR and AR on your speech delivery and identify areas for improvement.

11. **Stay Updated on Emerging Trends:**
   - Stay updated on emerging trends and advancements in VR and AR technology relevant to public speaking. Keep abreast of new platforms, tools, and applications that offer innovative ways to enhance speech delivery and audience engagement. Experiment with new features and functionalities to stay ahead of the curve and leverage the full potential of VR and AR in your presentations.

12. **Experiment and Innovate:**
   - Experiment with different approaches, techniques, and creative ideas for incorporating VR and AR into your speech delivery. Innovate and push the boundaries of what's possible with these technologies to create memorable and impactful presentations that resonate with your audience. Don't be afraid to think outside the box and explore new possibilities for immersive storytelling and communication.

Integrating Technology for Interactive Presentations

Integrating technology for interactive presentations is an excellent way to engage your audience and enhance the effectiveness of your public speaking. Here's a practical guide on how to effectively integrate technology for interactive presentations:

1. **Choose the Right Tools:**
   - Select interactive presentation tools and technologies that align with your objectives and audience preferences. Consider tools such as polling apps, audience response systems, interactive whiteboards, presentation software with built-in interactivity features, or virtual meeting platforms.

2. **Plan Your Interactive Elements:**
   - Plan interactive elements that will enhance audience engagement and participation throughout your presentation. This could include live polls, quizzes, surveys, interactive slides, virtual breakout sessions, Q&A sessions, interactive demos, or real-time audience feedback mechanisms.

3. Design Engaging Content:

- Design content that is visually appealing, dynamic, and tailored to the interactive format. Use multimedia elements such as images, videos, animations, and infographics to capture audience attention and reinforce key points. Create interactive slides with clickable buttons, hyperlinks, or embedded multimedia content.

4. Incorporate Live Polling and Quizzes:

- Incorporate live polling and quizzes into your presentation to gather real-time feedback and insights from your audience. Use polling apps or audience response systems to create interactive polls, multiple-choice questions, or quizzes that allow audience members to participate and provide input on relevant topics.

5. Encourage Audience Participation:

- Encourage audience participation throughout your presentation by inviting questions, comments, and contributions from the audience. Create opportunities for audience members to share their thoughts, experiences, or opinions on relevant topics. Foster a collaborative and inclusive atmosphere that encourages active engagement.

6. Facilitate Virtual Q&A Sessions:

- Facilitate virtual Q&A sessions where audience members can ask questions and interact with you as the speaker in real-time. Use chat features, live video feeds, or virtual meeting platforms to enable audience members to submit questions, comments, or feedback throughout the presentation.

7. Utilize Interactive Whiteboards:

- Utilize interactive whiteboards or digital collaboration tools to facilitate brainstorming sessions, idea sharing, or collaborative exercises during your presentation. Encourage audience members to contribute ideas, draw diagrams, or annotate slides in real-time using interactive whiteboard features.

8. Create Virtual Breakout Sessions:

- Create virtual breakout sessions or discussion groups where smaller groups of audience members can collaborate, share ideas, or work on interactive exercises. Use breakout room features in virtual meeting platforms to divide larger audiences into smaller groups for more focused discussions or activities.

9. Offer Hands-On Demos or Simulations:
- Offer hands-on demos or simulations that allow audience members to interact with your content in a tangible way. Use interactive simulations, virtual tours, or interactive demos to provide immersive experiences that enhance understanding and retention of key concepts.

10. Provide Real-Time Feedback:
- Provide real-time feedback to audience members during your presentation to acknowledge their contributions and address their questions or concerns. Use audience response systems or chat features to respond to audience inquiries, clarify points, or acknowledge insightful comments.

11. Test and Troubleshoot Technology:
- Test and troubleshoot all interactive elements and technology platforms before your presentation to ensure smooth operation and minimize technical issues. Conduct practice runs, simulate audience interactions, and familiarize yourself with the features and functionalities of your chosen tools.

12. Solicit Feedback and Evaluate:
- Solicit feedback from your audience after the presentation to evaluate the effectiveness of the interactive elements and gather insights for improvement. Use surveys, polls, or post-event discussions to gather feedback on the level of engagement, usefulness, and impact of the interactive features.

Chapter 15
Public Speaking and Leadership

The Intersection of Public Speaking and Leadership

The intersection of public speaking and leadership is profound, as effective communication lies at the core of leadership. Here's a practical guide on how public speaking and leadership intersect:

1. Inspiring and Motivating Others:
- Public speaking is a powerful tool for leaders to inspire and motivate others. Leaders who excel in public speaking can articulate a compelling vision, communicate values, and rally their team or audience behind a common purpose. Effective leaders use speeches and presentations to inspire action, foster enthusiasm, and drive positive change.

2. Building Trust and Credibility:
- Strong public speaking skills enhance a leader's ability to build trust and credibility with their team, stakeholders, and the wider community. Leaders who communicate confidently, authentically, and transparently establish credibility and earn the trust of their audience. They use speeches and presentations to demonstrate expertise, integrity, and sincerity, thereby strengthening relationships and fostering a culture of trust.

3. Setting Direction and Goals:
- Public speaking enables leaders to set direction, articulate goals, and communicate strategic priorities effectively. Leaders who can communicate a clear vision, set ambitious goals, and outline actionable plans inspire confidence and commitment from their team. They use speeches and presentations to align their audience around shared objectives, communicate expectations, and mobilize resources towards achieving common goals.

4. Driving Change and Innovation:
- Effective leaders use public speaking to drive change, promote innovation, and overcome resistance to new ideas. They communicate the need for change, articulate the benefits and opportunities, and address concerns or objections effectively. Leaders who can inspire confidence, optimism, and resilience through their speeches and

presentations foster a culture of innovation and continuous improvement within their organization.

5. Empowering and Developing Others:
   - Public speaking allows leaders to empower and develop others by providing guidance, feedback, and mentorship. Leaders who communicate with clarity, empathy, and encouragement create an environment where team members feel valued, supported, and empowered to grow and succeed. They use speeches and presentations to recognize achievements, provide constructive feedback, and inspire personal and professional development.

6. Navigating Challenges and Crises:
   - During challenging times or crises, public speaking becomes even more critical for leaders to reassure, inform, and guide their team or community. Leaders who can communicate calmly, confidently, and empathetically in the face of adversity inspire confidence and resilience. They use speeches and presentations to provide updates, address concerns, and offer guidance on navigating uncertain situations, thereby instilling a sense of stability and trust.

7. Building Relationships and Networks:
   - Public speaking provides leaders with opportunities to build relationships, expand networks, and cultivate partnerships. Leaders who are effective speakers can connect with diverse audiences, build rapport, and foster collaboration across teams, organizations, and communities. They use speeches and presentations to network, share insights, and engage with stakeholders, thereby strengthening relationships and enhancing their influence.

8. Leading by Example:
   - Public speaking allows leaders to lead by example and demonstrate key leadership qualities such as confidence, clarity, empathy, and resilience. Leaders who excel in public speaking set a positive example for their team, inspiring others to communicate effectively, embrace challenges, and strive for excellence. They use speeches and presentations to model desired behaviors, reinforce organizational values, and inspire others to follow their lead.

9. **Adapting to Diverse Audiences:**
   - Effective leaders are skilled at adapting their communication style and message to diverse audiences and situations. They tailor their speeches and presentations to resonate with different stakeholders, cultures, and contexts, demonstrating empathy, cultural awareness, and sensitivity. Leaders who can connect with diverse audiences through their public speaking build bridges, foster inclusion, and strengthen relationships across boundaries.

10. **Driving Organizational Success:**
   - Ultimately, the intersection of public speaking and leadership is about driving organizational success and achieving results. Leaders who master the art of public speaking can inspire, influence, and mobilize others towards a shared vision, strategic objectives, and collective goals. They use speeches and presentations strategically to lead their organization, drive performance, and create positive impact in the world.

Leading Effective Meetings and Discussions

Leading effective meetings and discussions is a vital aspect of public speaking and leadership. Here's a practical guide on how to lead such sessions with confidence:

1. **Set Clear Objectives:**
   - Before the meeting or discussion, define clear objectives outlining what you aim to achieve. Communicate these objectives to participants to provide focus and direction.

2. **Prepare an Agenda:**
   - Develop a structured agenda outlining topics to be covered, time allocations, and expected outcomes. Share the agenda in advance to allow participants to prepare.

3. **Engage Participants:**
   - Encourage active participation by engaging attendees in discussions, asking open-ended questions, and inviting input from all participants. Ensure everyone has the opportunity to contribute.

4. Manage Time Effectively:

- Keep discussions on track and manage time effectively to cover all agenda items. Set time limits for each topic and use gentle reminders to keep discussions focused.

5. Facilitate Constructive Dialogue:

- Foster an environment of open communication and constructive dialogue. Encourage respectful exchanges of ideas, diverse perspectives, and healthy debate while maintaining a positive atmosphere.

6. Listen Actively:

- Practice active listening by paying attention to what participants are saying, acknowledging their input, and seeking clarification when needed. Demonstrate empathy and understanding towards differing viewpoints.

7. Summarize Key Points:

- Summarize key points and decisions reached throughout the meeting to ensure clarity and alignment among participants. Confirm action items, responsibilities, and next steps before concluding the discussion.

8. Manage Group Dynamics:

- Be mindful of group dynamics and interpersonal relationships within the meeting. Address any conflicts or disruptions calmly and diplomatically to maintain a productive atmosphere.

9. Encourage Collaboration:

- Promote collaboration and teamwork by encouraging participants to build on each other's ideas, share expertise, and work towards common goals. Foster a sense of ownership and collective responsibility for outcomes.

10. Provide Leadership and Direction:

- As the meeting leader, provide clear leadership and direction to guide discussions towards productive outcomes. Offer insights, guidance, and expertise as needed while empowering others to contribute.

11. **Use Visual Aids Wisely:**
   - Utilize visual aids such as slides, charts, or diagrams to support discussions and convey complex information. Keep visuals clear, concise, and relevant to enhance understanding and engagement.

12. **Follow Up and Follow Through:**
   - After the meeting, follow up with participants to provide any additional information, clarify decisions, and reinforce action items. Ensure accountability by following through on commitments and monitoring progress towards goals.

Using Public Speaking Skills in Decision-Making

Using public speaking skills in decision-making is crucial for effective leadership. Here's a practical guide on how to leverage public speaking skills in decision-making processes:

1. **Clarity in Communication:**
   - When making decisions, articulate your thoughts clearly and concisely. Use public speaking skills such as clarity of speech, organization of ideas, and effective use of language to ensure everyone understands the decision-making process and the rationale behind your decisions.

2. **Engage Stakeholders:**
   - Engage stakeholders by involving them in the decision-making process through discussions, presentations, and feedback sessions. Use public speaking skills to facilitate dialogue, solicit input, and address concerns, ensuring that diverse perspectives are considered before making decisions.

3. **Presenting Options:**
   - Present various options or alternatives to decision-makers using persuasive communication techniques. Use public speaking skills such

as storytelling, persuasive language, and compelling arguments to advocate for specific options and influence decision outcomes.

4. Building Consensus:
- Use public speaking skills to build consensus among decision-makers by highlighting common ground, addressing objections, and finding mutually agreeable solutions. Foster a collaborative atmosphere where stakeholders feel empowered to contribute their ideas and perspectives.

5. Clarifying Complex Issues:
- Use public speaking skills to clarify complex issues and convey information effectively to decision-makers. Break down complex concepts into understandable terms, use analogies or examples to illustrate key points, and employ visual aids to enhance comprehension.

6. Addressing Resistance:
- Address resistance to proposed decisions by using public speaking skills to anticipate objections, acknowledge concerns, and provide reassurance. Use persuasive communication techniques to overcome resistance and gain buy-in from stakeholders.

7. Managing Conflicting Views:
- Use public speaking skills to manage conflicting views and foster constructive dialogue among decision-makers. Facilitate discussions, encourage active listening, and mediate disagreements to reach consensus and move the decision-making process forward.

8. Creating Buy-In:
- Use public speaking skills to create buy-in for decisions by effectively communicating the rationale, benefits, and potential outcomes to stakeholders. Use storytelling, emotional appeal, and logic to inspire confidence and enthusiasm for the chosen course of action.

9. Presenting Recommendations:
- Present recommendations or decisions to stakeholders with confidence and conviction. Use public speaking skills to deliver

persuasive presentations, address questions or concerns, and reinforce the importance of the chosen course of action.

10. Seeking Feedback:

- Use public speaking skills to seek feedback from stakeholders on decisions made and the decision-making process itself. Conduct post-decision debriefings, feedback sessions, or surveys to gather insights, identify areas for improvement, and foster continuous learning and improvement.

11. Adapting Communication Style:

- Adapt your communication style to suit the preferences and needs of different decision-makers and stakeholders. Use public speaking skills to tailor your message, tone, and delivery to effectively engage and influence diverse audiences.

12. Demonstrating Confidence and Authority:

- Use public speaking skills to demonstrate confidence, authority, and credibility in decision-making processes. Project confidence through your body language, tone of voice, and demeanor, and communicate decisiveness and clarity in your decisions.

Motivating and Inspiring Through Speech

Motivating and inspiring through speech is a fundamental aspect of effective leadership. Here's a practical guide on how to leverage public speaking skills to motivate and inspire others:

1. Know Your Audience:

- Understand the motivations, interests, and aspirations of your audience. Tailor your speech to resonate with their values, goals, and emotions to increase the likelihood of inspiring them.

2. Craft a Compelling Narrative:

- Develop a compelling narrative that captures the imagination and emotions of your audience. Use storytelling techniques to convey your message in a memorable and relatable way, making it easier for listeners to connect with your speech.

3. Start with a Strong Opening:

- Capture attention from the outset with a powerful opening that sets the tone for your speech. Use attention-grabbing anecdotes, quotes, or questions to pique curiosity and draw listeners in.

4. Communicate Vision and Purpose:

- Clearly articulate your vision, purpose, and goals to inspire others to action. Paint a vivid picture of the future you envision and explain how each individual's contributions are essential to achieving that vision.

5. Use Inspirational Language:

- Use language that evokes emotion and inspires action. Use words and phrases that convey optimism, hope, and possibility, reinforcing the belief that positive change is achievable.

6. Demonstrate Authenticity and Passion:

- Speak authentically and passionately about your beliefs and convictions. Let your enthusiasm and sincerity shine through in your speech, as genuine passion is contagious and inspires others to follow your lead.

7. Provide Concrete Examples and Stories:

- Illustrate your points with concrete examples and real-life stories that demonstrate the impact of your message. Personal anecdotes and success stories can make abstract concepts more tangible and relatable to your audience.

8. Use Powerful Imagery and Metaphors:

- Use vivid imagery and metaphors to paint a vivid picture in the minds of your audience. Analogies and metaphors can help simplify complex ideas and make them easier to understand and remember.

9. Engage the Audience Emotionally:

- Appeal to the emotions of your audience by speaking to their hopes, fears, and aspirations. Use emotional storytelling, humor, or personal anecdotes to forge a deep emotional connection with your listeners.

10. **Empower and Encourage Action:**
   - Empower your audience by providing practical steps they can take to turn inspiration into action. Encourage them to set goals, overcome obstacles, and pursue their dreams with confidence and determination.

11. **Use Dynamic Delivery Techniques:**
   - Use dynamic delivery techniques such as varying your tone, pacing, and volume to keep your audience engaged and captivated. Use gestures, facial expressions, and body language to convey enthusiasm and conviction.

12. **End with a Strong Call to Action:**
   - End your speech with a strong call to action that inspires listeners to take immediate steps towards positive change. Encourage them to embrace new opportunities, overcome challenges, and work together towards a common goal.

Building a Leadership Brand through Public Speaking

Building a leadership brand through public speaking is a powerful way to establish credibility, influence, and authority. Here's a practical guide on how to leverage public speaking to build your leadership brand:

1. Define Your Leadership Brand:
   - Start by defining your leadership brand—what sets you apart as a leader and what values, qualities, and expertise you want to be known for. Your leadership brand should align with your personal and professional goals and resonate with your target audience.

2. Identify Your Core Messages:
   - Identify the key messages you want to convey through your public speaking engagements. These messages should reflect your leadership brand, highlight your unique strengths and perspectives, and communicate your vision and values to your audience.

3. Establish Thought Leadership:

 - Use public speaking as a platform to establish yourself as a thought leader in your field. Share insights, expertise, and innovative ideas that demonstrate your knowledge and expertise, and position yourself as a trusted authority on relevant topics.

4. Develop Your Speaking Style:

 - Develop a speaking style that reflects your leadership brand and resonates with your audience. Whether you prefer a charismatic, authoritative, or empathetic approach, ensure that your speaking style aligns with your personality and leadership style.

5. Craft Compelling Presentations:

 - Craft compelling presentations that showcase your expertise, insights, and unique perspective. Use storytelling, data, examples, and visuals to engage your audience, convey your message effectively, and leave a lasting impression.

6. Engage with Your Audience:

 - Engage with your audience before, during, and after your speeches to build rapport, establish connections, and foster relationships. Encourage interaction, invite questions and feedback, and be approachable and accessible to your audience.

7. Consistency and Authenticity:

 - Be consistent in your messaging and authentic in your delivery. Your leadership brand should shine through in every public speaking engagement, reinforcing your values, beliefs, and leadership style with every interaction.

8. Leverage Social Media and Online Platforms:

 - Use social media and online platforms to amplify your leadership brand and reach a broader audience. Share insights, thought leadership content, and updates about your speaking engagements to establish your presence as a leader in your industry.

9. Seek Speaking Opportunities:

- Proactively seek out speaking opportunities at conferences, industry events, webinars, podcasts, and other platforms where you can showcase your expertise and leadership brand. Be strategic in choosing events that align with your brand and target audience.

10. Build a Strong Personal Brand:

- Invest in building a strong personal brand that complements your leadership brand. Develop a professional online presence, create a compelling bio, and curate content that reinforces your expertise, values, and leadership style.

11. Seek Feedback and Continuous Improvement:

- Seek feedback from your audience, peers, and mentors to continuously refine and improve your public speaking skills and leadership brand. Act on constructive feedback and embrace opportunities for growth and development.

12. Lead by Example:

- Finally, lead by example and embody the qualities and values that define your leadership brand. Demonstrate integrity, authenticity, and commitment to excellence in everything you do, both on and off the stage.

Chapter 16
Public Speaking Across Cultures

Cultural Sensitivity in Speech Preparation

Cultural sensitivity in speech preparation is essential for effective public speaking across cultures. Here's a practical guide on how to ensure cultural sensitivity when preparing speeches:

1. **Research Your Audience:**
   - Start by researching your audience's cultural background, values, customs, and communication preferences. Understand their cultural norms regarding topics such as humor, formality, and social etiquette to tailor your speech accordingly.

2. **Avoid Assumptions and Stereotypes:**
   - Avoid making assumptions or relying on stereotypes about cultural groups. Recognize the diversity within cultures and avoid generalizations that may inadvertently offend or misrepresent your audience.

3. **Respect Cultural Differences:**
   - Respect cultural differences and show sensitivity to cultural norms and practices. Be mindful of topics that may be considered taboo or sensitive in certain cultures and avoid inadvertently causing offense.

4. **Adapt Your Language and Content:**
   - Adapt your language and content to be inclusive and accessible to a diverse audience. Use clear, straightforward language and avoid jargon, idioms, or cultural references that may be unfamiliar or confusing to some listeners.

5. **Consider Non-Verbal Communication:**
   - Pay attention to non-verbal communication cues such as body language, gestures, and facial expressions that may vary across cultures. Be aware of cultural differences in eye contact, personal space, and other non-verbal signals, and adjust your own behavior accordingly.

6. **Acknowledge Cultural Diversity:**
   - Acknowledge and celebrate cultural diversity in your speech by incorporating examples, stories, or references that reflect the richness

of different cultures. Demonstrate inclusivity and respect for all cultural backgrounds represented in your audience.

7. Seek Feedback from Cultural Insiders:

- Seek feedback from individuals who have cultural insight or expertise relevant to your audience. Consult with cultural insiders, such as colleagues, friends, or cultural advisors, to ensure that your speech is culturally appropriate and respectful.

8. Adapt to Cultural Sensitivities:

- Adapt your speech to accommodate cultural sensitivities or taboos that may exist within certain cultures. Avoid topics or language that may be considered offensive, controversial, or disrespectful, and be prepared to adjust your content as needed.

9. Address Cultural Context:

- Address the cultural context of your audience in your speech by acknowledging shared experiences, values, or challenges. Tailor your examples and anecdotes to resonate with the cultural background and context of your listeners.

10. Practice Cross-Cultural Communication:

- Practice cross-cultural communication skills to enhance your ability to connect with diverse audiences. Be open-minded, empathetic, and adaptable in your interactions, and demonstrate a willingness to learn from and engage with different cultural perspectives.

11. Be Open to Feedback:

- Be open to feedback from your audience regarding the cultural appropriateness and effectiveness of your speech. Use feedback as an opportunity to learn and improve your cross-cultural communication skills for future speaking engagements.

12. Reflect on Cultural Sensitivity:

- Reflect on your own cultural biases, assumptions, and blind spots to continuously improve your cultural sensitivity in speech preparation. Cultivate a mindset of curiosity, humility, and respect for cultural differences as you strive to become a more effective cross-cultural communicator.

Adapting Communication Styles to Cultural Norms

Adapting communication styles to cultural norms is crucial for successful public speaking across cultures. Here's a practical guide on how to adapt your communication style to effectively engage with diverse cultural audiences:

1. **Understand Cultural Communication Styles:**
   - Begin by understanding the communication styles prevalent in the cultures you will be addressing. Some cultures may value directness and assertiveness, while others prioritize indirectness and diplomacy. Research cultural communication norms to adapt your style accordingly.

2. **Observe and Listen:**
   - Pay attention to how people from different cultural backgrounds communicate in various contexts. Observe their use of language, tone, body language, and interpersonal dynamics to gain insights into cultural communication norms.

3. **Respect Hierarchy and Authority:**
   - Be mindful of hierarchical structures and authority dynamics that may exist within certain cultures. In cultures with strong hierarchical norms, demonstrate respect for authority figures and use appropriate forms of address and deference in your communication.

4. **Tailor Your Language and Tone:**
   - Tailor your language and tone to match the cultural preferences of your audience. Use language that is clear, concise, and respectful, and adjust your tone to reflect the level of formality or informality expected in the cultural context.

5. **Adjust Non-Verbal Communication:**
   - Adapt your non-verbal communication, including body language, gestures, and facial expressions, to align with cultural norms. Be mindful of differences in personal space, eye contact, and physical touch, and adjust your behavior accordingly.

6. Be Mindful of Time Orientation:

- Consider cultural attitudes towards time and punctuality when planning and delivering your speech. In some cultures, timeliness is highly valued, while in others, a more relaxed approach to time may be the norm. Be respectful of cultural attitudes towards time and adjust your schedule and pacing accordingly.

7. Use Stories and Analogies:

- Use stories, analogies, and metaphors that resonate with the cultural background and experiences of your audience. Draw on cultural references and examples to make your message more relatable and engaging to listeners from diverse cultural backgrounds.

8. Encourage Participation and Collaboration:

- Adapt your speaking style to encourage participation and collaboration in accordance with cultural norms. In some cultures, group consensus and collective decision-making may be preferred, while in others, individual contributions and assertiveness may be valued.

9. Show Cultural Sensitivity and Respect:

- Demonstrate cultural sensitivity and respect in your communication by avoiding language or behavior that may be perceived as offensive, disrespectful, or insensitive. Be open-minded, curious, and empathetic towards different cultural perspectives and values.

10. Seek Feedback and Adjustments:

- Seek feedback from members of the cultural group you are addressing to assess the effectiveness of your communication style. Be willing to make adjustments and adaptations based on feedback to ensure that your message resonates with your audience.

11. Build Relationships and Trust:

- Focus on building relationships and trust with your audience by demonstrating authenticity, empathy, and cultural competence in your communication. Show genuine interest in the cultural background and experiences of your listeners to foster connection and rapport.

12. **Continuously Learn and Adapt:**
   - Continuously learn about different cultural communication styles
and adapt your approach based on the specific cultural context of each
speaking engagement. Embrace opportunities for cross-cultural
learning and growth to become a more effective communicator across
cultures.

Language Considerations in Multicultural Audiences

When addressing multicultural audiences, language considerations play
a crucial role in ensuring effective communication. Here's a practical
guide on navigating language considerations in public speaking across
cultures:

1. **Identify Language Preferences:**
   - Determine the primary language or languages spoken by your
audience. Consider whether interpretation services are needed and
ensure that language barriers are addressed to facilitate
understanding.

2. **Use Clear and Simple Language:**
   - Choose clear and straightforward language to ensure comprehension
across language barriers. Avoid jargon, slang, or complex terminology
that may be difficult for non-native speakers to understand.

3. **Provide Translation and Interpretation Services:**
   - If addressing an audience with diverse language backgrounds,
provide translation or interpretation services to accommodate different
language preferences. Ensure that translated materials and
interpreters are proficient in the target languages and accurately
convey your message.

4. **Offer Multilingual Materials:**
   - Provide written materials, such as slides, handouts, or
presentations, in multiple languages to cater to diverse language

preferences. This demonstrates inclusivity and ensures that all audience members can access the information presented.

5. Use Visual Aids and Graphics:
   - Utilize visual aids, graphics, and images to supplement verbal communication and enhance understanding, particularly for audience members with limited proficiency in the spoken language. Visuals can help convey key concepts and messages effectively across language barriers.

6. Speak Slowly and Clearly:
   - Speak at a moderate pace and enunciate clearly to aid comprehension, especially for non-native speakers of the language. Avoid speaking too fast or using colloquialisms that may be challenging for non-native speakers to follow.

7. Encourage Participation and Clarification:
   - Encourage audience participation and provide opportunities for clarification or questions, particularly for audience members who may be struggling with language comprehension. Be patient and receptive to inquiries, and ensure that all questions are addressed adequately.

8. Be Mindful of Cultural Nuances:
   - Consider cultural nuances and sensitivities that may impact language comprehension. Be mindful of linguistic variations, idiomatic expressions, and cultural references that may require explanation or clarification for audience members from different cultural backgrounds.

9. Provide Pre-Event Language Support:
   - Offer pre-event language support, such as language primers or glossaries, to help audience members familiarize themselves with key terminology and concepts in advance. This can enhance comprehension and engagement during the presentation.

10. Adapt to Multilingual Audiences:
   - Adapt your speaking style and delivery to accommodate multilingual audiences. Use repetition, visual cues, and other communication techniques to reinforce key messages and ensure that

all audience members can follow along regardless of language proficiency.

11. **Seek Feedback and Adjustments:**
   - Solicit feedback from audience members regarding language accessibility and comprehension. Use feedback to make adjustments and improvements to future presentations, ensuring that language considerations are effectively addressed.

12. **Promote Language Learning and Inclusivity:**
   - Foster a culture of language learning and inclusivity within your speaking engagements. Encourage audience members to engage with different languages and cultures, and strive to create an environment where everyone feels valued and included.

Building Global Connection Through Public Speaking

Building global connections through public speaking involves fostering understanding, empathy, and collaboration across diverse cultural boundaries. Here's a practical guide on how to achieve this:

1. **Cultural Awareness and Sensitivity:**
   - Develop cultural awareness and sensitivity to understand the nuances and diversity of cultures around the world. Recognize and respect cultural differences, values, and communication styles to bridge cultural divides effectively.

2. **Research Your Audience:**
   - Research the cultural backgrounds, preferences, and communication norms of your global audience. Tailor your message and delivery to resonate with their cultural sensibilities and address topics that are relevant and meaningful to them.

3. **Use Universal Themes and Values:**
   - Focus on universal themes and values that transcend cultural boundaries, such as empathy, collaboration, and innovation. Frame

your message in a way that resonates with people from diverse backgrounds and fosters a sense of common humanity.

4. Promote Diversity and Inclusion:
- Champion diversity and inclusion in your public speaking engagements by highlighting the importance of diverse perspectives and experiences. Encourage dialogue and collaboration among individuals from different cultural backgrounds to foster mutual understanding and respect.

5. Share Personal Stories and Experiences:
- Share personal stories and experiences that illustrate common challenges, triumphs, and aspirations shared by people around the world. Authentic storytelling can build empathy, forge connections, and break down cultural barriers.

6. Facilitate Cross-Cultural Dialogue:
- Create opportunities for cross-cultural dialogue and exchange of ideas by organizing multicultural events, conferences, or panel discussions. Encourage participants to share their perspectives, insights, and solutions to global challenges.

7. Utilize Technology for Global Reach:
- Leverage technology, such as live streaming, webinars, and virtual events, to reach global audiences and facilitate cross-cultural communication. Use interactive tools and platforms to engage with participants from different parts of the world in real-time.

8. Encourage Language Learning and Exchange:
- Encourage language learning and exchange among your audience members to promote linguistic diversity and cultural understanding. Provide resources, support, and opportunities for language practice and cross-cultural communication.

9. Collaborate with Global Partners:
- Collaborate with global organizations, institutions, or speakers to co-create content and initiatives that promote global connection and understanding. Pool resources, expertise, and networks to reach diverse audiences and amplify your impact.

10. **Embrace Cultural Exchange and Immersion:**
   - Embrace opportunities for cultural exchange and immersion by participating in international conferences, workshops, or study abroad programs. Immerse yourself in different cultures, languages, and ways of thinking to broaden your perspective and deepen your global connections.

11. **Seek Feedback and Continuous Improvement:**
   - Solicit feedback from your global audience to assess the effectiveness of your communication efforts and identify areas for improvement. Use feedback to refine your approach and tailor your message to better resonate with diverse cultural audiences.

12. **Lead by Example:**
   - Lead by example as a global citizen committed to fostering understanding, empathy, and collaboration across borders. Demonstrate openness, curiosity, and respect for cultural diversity in your interactions and initiatives, inspiring others to do the same.

Navigating Cross-Cultural Communication Challenges

Navigating cross-cultural communication challenges requires sensitivity, adaptability, and a deep understanding of cultural differences. Here's a practical guide on how to effectively navigate these challenges in public speaking:

1. **Cultural Research and Awareness:**
   - Conduct thorough research on the cultural backgrounds, norms, values, and communication styles of your audience. Develop a keen awareness of cultural differences and similarities to anticipate potential communication challenges.

2. **Avoid Assumptions and Stereotypes:**
   - Avoid making assumptions or relying on stereotypes about cultural groups. Recognize that cultural norms and behaviors vary widely, and

individuals may not necessarily conform to stereotypes associated with
their cultural background.

3. Adapt Communication Style:
   - Adapt your communication style to accommodate the cultural
preferences of your audience. Be mindful of differences in language
use, nonverbal communication, and interpersonal interactions, and
adjust your approach accordingly.

4. Clarify Misunderstandings:
   - Be proactive in clarifying misunderstandings and addressing cultural
differences that may arise during your speech. Encourage open
dialogue, ask clarifying questions, and seek feedback to ensure that
your message is accurately understood.

5. Bridge Language Barriers:
   - Address language barriers by using simple and clear language,
avoiding jargon or complex terminology, and providing translation or
interpretation services when necessary. Use visual aids, gestures, and
repetition to reinforce key points and enhance comprehension.

6. Respect Cultural Sensitivities:
   - Show respect for cultural sensitivities and taboos by avoiding topics
or language that may be considered offensive or inappropriate in
certain cultures. Be mindful of religious, political, or social issues that
may be sensitive or contentious.

7. Practice Active Listening:
   - Practice active listening to understand the perspectives and
concerns of individuals from different cultural backgrounds. Be
attentive, empathetic, and nonjudgmental in your interactions, and
demonstrate genuine interest in learning from others.

8. Manage Conflict Constructively:
   - Handle conflicts or disagreements that may arise due to cultural
differences with tact and diplomacy. Seek common ground, focus on
areas of agreement, and strive to find mutually acceptable solutions
that respect the cultural values and perspectives of all parties
involved.

9. Build Trust and Rapport:

- Invest time and effort in building trust and rapport with your audience by demonstrating authenticity, empathy, and cultural competence. Show appreciation for cultural diversity and foster a sense of inclusivity and belonging in your interactions.

10. Embrace Cultural Diversity:

- Embrace cultural diversity as an opportunity for learning, growth, and collaboration. Celebrate the richness and variety of cultural perspectives and experiences, and encourage cross-cultural exchange and dialogue in your speaking engagements.

11. Seek Feedback and Learn from Experience:

- Seek feedback from your audience and peers to gain insights into your effectiveness in navigating cross-cultural communication challenges. Reflect on your experiences, learn from mistakes, and continuously refine your approach to better connect with diverse audiences.

12. Cultivate Cultural Competence:

- Cultivate cultural competence by actively seeking to understand and appreciate different cultural perspectives, values, and communication styles. Invest in cultural sensitivity training, cross-cultural communication workshops, and other resources to enhance your ability to navigate cross-cultural communication challenges effectively.

Chapter 17
Public Speaking and
Personal Branding

The Role of Public Speaking in Personal Branding

Public speaking plays a significant role in shaping and enhancing personal branding. Here's how:

1. **Establishing Expertise and Authority:**
   - Public speaking allows individuals to showcase their knowledge, expertise, and insights on specific topics. By delivering engaging and informative presentations, speakers can establish themselves as thought leaders in their respective fields, building credibility and authority within their industry.

2. **Building Trust and Credibility:**
   - Effective public speaking helps to build trust and credibility with the audience. When speakers deliver compelling and well-researched presentations, they demonstrate their expertise and professionalism, earning the trust and respect of their listeners. This trust is essential for building a strong personal brand.

3. **Differentiation from Competitors:**
   - Public speaking offers an opportunity for individuals to differentiate themselves from competitors within their industry. By delivering unique and insightful presentations, speakers can stand out as distinctive voices in their field, enhancing their personal brand and attracting attention from potential clients, employers, or collaborators.

4. **Creating a Memorable Impression:**
   - Engaging public speaking allows individuals to create a memorable impression on their audience. Through compelling storytelling, persuasive arguments, and dynamic delivery, speakers can leave a lasting impact on listeners, reinforcing their personal brand and increasing their visibility and influence.

5. **Networking and Relationship Building:**
   - Public speaking provides a platform for networking and relationship building with like-minded professionals, industry peers, and potential clients or collaborators. By delivering impactful presentations at conferences, seminars, or networking events, speakers can expand

their professional network and enhance their personal brand through meaningful connections.

6. Enhancing Visibility and Exposure:

- Public speaking offers an opportunity for individuals to increase their visibility and exposure within their industry and beyond. By speaking at conferences, events, or webinars, speakers can reach a wider audience and attract attention to their expertise, accomplishments, and unique value proposition, further strengthening their personal brand.

7. Demonstrating Communication Skills:

- Public speaking serves as a powerful demonstration of an individual's communication skills and abilities. By delivering polished and articulate presentations, speakers showcase their ability to convey complex ideas, engage an audience, and inspire action, enhancing their personal brand as effective communicators and influencers.

8. Reinforcing Brand Values and Messaging:

- Public speaking allows individuals to reinforce their personal brand values and messaging through their presentations. By aligning their speaking topics and content with their brand identity and values, speakers can create a cohesive and authentic brand narrative that resonates with their audience and strengthens their brand image.

9. Generating Opportunities:

- Effective public speaking can lead to various opportunities, including media interviews, guest appearances, consulting engagements, or career advancements. By consistently delivering high-quality presentations and showcasing their expertise, speakers can attract new opportunities that further enhance their personal brand and professional success.

10. Continued Growth and Development:

- Public speaking provides a platform for continued growth and development as individuals refine their presentation skills, expand their knowledge, and explore new topics and areas of interest. By actively engaging in public speaking opportunities, speakers can continuously evolve and strengthen their personal brand over time.

Aligning Your Message with Your Brand

Aligning your message with your personal brand is essential for effective public speaking. Here's a practical guide on how to ensure consistency and alignment between your message and your brand:

1. **Define Your Personal Brand:**
   - Start by defining your personal brand identity, including your values, strengths, expertise, and unique selling points. Clarify what sets you apart from others and what you want to be known for in your industry or field.

2. **Identify Key Messaging:**
   - Identify key messages that reflect your personal brand and resonate with your target audience. These messages should encapsulate your core values, expertise, and the benefits you offer to your audience.

3. **Understand Your Audience:**
   - Gain a deep understanding of your audience, including their needs, interests, preferences, and pain points. Tailor your message to address their specific concerns and provide value that aligns with their expectations.

4. **Craft Compelling Stories:**
   - Use storytelling techniques to convey your personal brand message in a compelling and relatable way. Share personal anecdotes, case studies, or examples that illustrate your values, experiences, and achievements, and connect with your audience on an emotional level.

5. **Stay Authentic and Genuine:**
   - Authenticity is key to building trust and credibility with your audience. Ensure that your message reflects your genuine personality, beliefs, and experiences, and avoid trying to be someone you're not. Authenticity resonates with audiences and strengthens your personal brand.

6. **Communicate Consistently:**

- Maintain consistency in your communication across different
channels and platforms. Ensure that your message is aligned with your
personal brand identity and values, whether you're speaking at events,
writing articles, or engaging on social media.

7. Use Visual Branding Elements:
- Incorporate visual branding elements into your presentations, such
as your logo, colors, and design aesthetics, to reinforce your personal
brand identity. Consistent visual branding helps to create a cohesive
and recognizable brand image.

8. Focus on Your Unique Value Proposition:
- Highlight your unique value proposition in your message to
differentiate yourself from others in your industry. Clearly articulate
what sets you apart and why your audience should pay attention to
what you have to say.

9. Be Strategic in Your Messaging:
- Be strategic in your messaging by focusing on topics and themes
that align with your personal brand and resonate with your audience.
Choose content that showcases your expertise and positions you as a
credible authority in your field.

10. Seek Feedback and Refine:
- Solicit feedback from trusted colleagues, mentors, or audience
members to ensure that your message effectively aligns with your
personal brand. Use feedback to refine and improve your messaging
over time, continuously strengthening your brand identity.

11. Monitor Your Brand Perception:
- Monitor how your audience perceives your personal brand and
adjust your messaging as needed to address any discrepancies or areas
for improvement. Regularly evaluate the alignment between your
message and your brand identity to maintain consistency and
relevance.

12. Stay True to Your Brand Values:
- Stay true to your brand values and principles, even as you evolve
and grow in your public speaking endeavors. Your message should

always reflect your authentic self and uphold the values that define your personal brand.

Developing a Unique Speaking Style

Developing a unique speaking style is crucial for building a strong personal brand in public speaking. Here's a practical guide on how to develop a distinctive speaking style that reflects your personality, resonates with your audience, and strengthens your personal brand:

1. **Know Yourself:**
   - Start by understanding your personality, strengths, and natural communication style. Identify what makes you unique as a speaker and leverage those qualities to develop your speaking style.

2. **Define Your Brand Identity:**
   - Clarify your personal brand identity, including your values, goals, and the image you want to project to your audience. Your speaking style should align with your brand identity and reinforce the key messages you want to convey.

3. **Study Other Speakers:**
   - Study other speakers, both within and outside your industry, to gain inspiration and insights into different speaking styles. Observe how they engage their audience, use language, and convey their message, and identify elements that resonate with you.

4. **Practice Regularly:**
   - Practice speaking regularly to hone your skills and refine your style. Experiment with different techniques, delivery methods, and presentation formats to discover what works best for you and what feels most authentic.

5. **Embrace Authenticity:**
   - Embrace authenticity in your speaking style by being true to yourself and expressing your genuine personality. Authenticity builds trust and connection with your audience and sets you apart from speakers who try to imitate others.

6. Find Your Voice:

   - Develop your unique voice as a speaker by finding a tone, cadence, and rhythm that feel comfortable and natural to you. Your voice is a powerful tool for conveying emotion, emphasis, and personality in your presentations.

7. Use Storytelling:

   - Incorporate storytelling into your speeches to engage your audience and make your message more memorable. Share personal anecdotes, experiences, and examples that illustrate your key points and captivate your audience's attention.

8. Master Nonverbal Communication:

   - Pay attention to your nonverbal communication, including your body language, gestures, and facial expressions. Nonverbal cues can convey confidence, enthusiasm, and authenticity, enhancing your speaking style and reinforcing your message.

9. Adapt to Your Audience:

   - Adapt your speaking style to suit the preferences and expectations of your audience. Consider factors such as their age, background, culture, and level of expertise, and tailor your delivery accordingly to maximize impact and resonance.

10. Seek Feedback:

   - Solicit feedback from trusted mentors, colleagues, or audience members to gain insights into your speaking style and areas for improvement. Use feedback to refine your approach and make adjustments that align with your personal brand.

11. Be Flexible and Versatile:

   - Be flexible and versatile in your speaking style, adapting to different speaking environments, topics, and audiences as needed. Develop the ability to switch between formal and informal styles, as well as adjust your pace and tone to suit the context.

12. Continuously Evolve:

- Continuously evolve and refine your speaking style over time, incorporating feedback, learning from experience, and pushing yourself outside your comfort zone. Your speaking style should grow and adapt as you gain confidence and experience as a speaker.

Leveraging Public Speaking for Career Advancement

Leveraging public speaking for career advancement can be a strategic way to showcase your expertise, build credibility, and expand your professional network. Here's a practical guide on how to use public speaking to advance your career:

1. **Identify Your Career Goals:**
   - Start by clarifying your career goals and objectives. Determine the skills, knowledge, and experiences you need to achieve your career aspirations, and identify how public speaking can support your professional development.

2. **Define Your Expertise:**
   - Identify your areas of expertise and subject matter knowledge that you can leverage in your public speaking engagements. Highlight your unique insights, experiences, and perspectives that set you apart as a thought leader in your field.

3. **Seek Speaking Opportunities:**
   - Actively seek speaking opportunities within your industry, professional associations, academic institutions, or community organizations. Look for conferences, seminars, workshops, panel discussions, or networking events where you can share your expertise and insights with a relevant audience.

4. **Pitch Yourself as a Speaker:**
   - Develop a compelling speaker pitch that highlights your expertise, speaking topics, and the value you can bring to an audience. Tailor your pitch to the specific event or organization you're targeting,

emphasizing how your presentation will benefit their audience and align with their objectives.

5. Build Your Speaker Profile:
   - Create a professional speaker profile that showcases your expertise, credentials, speaking experience, and testimonials from previous engagements. Use your speaker profile to promote yourself to event organizers, conference planners, and potential collaborators.

6. Craft Engaging Presentations:
   - Develop engaging and informative presentations that showcase your expertise and provide value to your audience. Tailor your content to address the needs, interests, and challenges of your target audience, and use storytelling, visuals, and interactive elements to captivate their attention.

7. Network with Industry Professionals:
   - Network with industry professionals, influencers, and decision-makers within your field through your public speaking engagements. Use speaking opportunities as a platform to connect with key stakeholders, establish relationships, and expand your professional network.

8. Share Your Successes:
   - Share your speaking successes and accomplishments with your professional network and on your online platforms, or your personal website. Highlight any positive feedback, testimonials, or recognition you've received as a speaker to enhance your credibility and visibility.

9. Develop Thought Leadership Content:
   - Create thought leadership content, such as articles, blog posts, podcasts, or videos, that complement your public speaking presentations and reinforce your expertise. Share your content with your audience to demonstrate your knowledge and insights on relevant industry topics.

10. Continuously Improve Your Skills:
   - Invest in continuous learning and skill development to enhance your public speaking abilities. Take courses, workshops, or coaching

sessions to improve your presentation skills, overcome any challenges or weaknesses, and refine your speaking style.

11. Measure Your Impact:
- Evaluate the impact of your public speaking engagements on your career advancement goals. Track metrics such as speaking opportunities secured, audience engagement levels, networking connections made, and career opportunities generated as a result of your speaking engagements.

12. Stay Persistent and Resilient:
- Be persistent and resilient in pursuing speaking opportunities and advancing your career through public speaking. Rejection and setbacks are part of the process, but with perseverance and dedication, you can leverage public speaking to achieve your career goals and make a meaningful impact in your field.

Measuring the Impact of Your Public Speaking Brand

Measuring the impact of your public speaking brand is essential for understanding your effectiveness as a speaker, identifying areas for improvement, and maximizing your influence. Here's a practical guide on how to measure the impact of your public speaking brand:

1. Set Clear Objectives:
- Start by setting clear objectives for your public speaking brand. Determine what you aim to achieve through your speaking engagements, whether it's building credibility, expanding your network, generating leads, or increasing visibility in your industry.

2. Define Key Performance Indicators (KPIs):
- Identify key performance indicators (KPIs) that align with your objectives and can be used to measure the impact of your public speaking brand. Examples of KPIs include the number of speaking engagements secured, audience engagement levels, feedback ratings,

leads generated, or opportunities generated as a result of your speaking engagements.

3. Track Speaking Engagements:
- Keep track of all your speaking engagements, including the event name, date, location, audience size, topic, and format. Use a spreadsheet or a dedicated tracking tool to maintain a comprehensive record of your speaking activities.

4. Collect Feedback and Testimonials:
- Collect feedback and testimonials from event organizers, audience members, and participants after each speaking engagement. Use surveys, feedback forms, or follow-up emails to gather insights on the impact of your presentation, the relevance of your content, and the effectiveness of your delivery.

5. Monitor Online Engagement:
- Monitor online engagement related to your speaking engagements, such as social media mentions, shares, likes, comments, or website traffic generated from your presentations. Analyze the reach and engagement metrics to gauge the level of interest and interaction with your content.

6. Evaluate Audience Engagement:
- Evaluate audience engagement during your presentations by observing their reactions, interactions, and participation levels. Pay attention to nonverbal cues, such as body language, facial expressions, and applause, to assess the level of audience engagement and interest in your message.

7. Analyze Lead Generation and Conversion:
- Analyze the impact of your speaking engagements on lead generation and conversion by tracking the number of leads generated, inquiries received, or business opportunities generated as a result of your presentations. Measure the conversion rate of leads into clients, customers, or collaborators to assess the effectiveness of your speaking brand in driving business outcomes.

8. Assess Brand Recognition and Visibility:

- Assess your brand recognition and visibility within your industry or target audience by monitoring mentions, references, or citations of your name or brand in relevant publications, media coverage, or online discussions. Measure the increase in brand awareness and visibility as a result of your speaking engagements.

9. Review Performance Against Objectives:

- Regularly review your performance against your objectives and KPIs to assess the impact of your public speaking brand. Identify areas of strength and areas for improvement, and adjust your strategy and approach accordingly to optimize your impact as a speaker.

10. Seek Input from Stakeholders:

- Seek input from stakeholders, such as event organizers, industry peers, or mentors, to gain additional perspectives on the impact of your public speaking brand. Incorporate their feedback and insights into your evaluation process to ensure a comprehensive assessment of your speaking effectiveness.

11. Iterate and Improve:

- Use the insights gained from your measurement efforts to iterate and improve your public speaking brand over time. Identify areas where you can enhance your effectiveness as a speaker, refine your messaging, or expand your reach to achieve greater impact and influence.

12. Celebrate Successes and Milestones:

- Celebrate your successes and milestones as a speaker, whether it's securing a high-profile speaking engagement, receiving positive feedback from your audience, or achieving significant results from your presentations. Acknowledge your achievements and use them as motivation to continue growing and evolving as a speaker.

Chapter 18
Public Speaking in the Digital Age

Online Platforms for Public Speaking

In the digital age, there are numerous online platforms that offer opportunities for public speaking and reaching audiences worldwide. Here's a practical guide to some of the key online platforms you can leverage for public speaking:

1. **Webinars and Virtual Events:**
   - Webinars and virtual events provide a platform for delivering presentations, workshops, or panel discussions to remote audiences. Platforms offer features for hosting live online events with interactive Q&A sessions, polls, and audience engagement tools.

2. **Podcasting Platforms:**
   - Podcasting platforms enable you to host and produce audio-based content, such as interviews, discussions, or educational episodes. Platforms allow you to create and distribute your podcasts to a global audience, reaching listeners on various streaming platforms.

3. **Video Sharing Platforms:**
   - Video sharing platforms offer opportunities for public speaking through recorded video content. You can create and upload videos of your presentations, speeches, or tutorials to reach a wide audience of viewers. Platforms provide tools for hosting, sharing, and monetizing your video content.

4. **Live Streaming Platforms:**
   - Live streaming platforms allow you to broadcast live video content to audiences in real-time. Platforms enable you to engage with viewers through live chats, comments, and reactions while delivering your speech or presentation.

5. **Online Conferences and Summits:**
   - Online conferences and summits bring together speakers and attendees from around the world to discuss and share insights on specific topics or industries. Platforms offer virtual event solutions that include features for hosting keynote presentations, breakout sessions, networking activities, and exhibitor booths.

6. Social Media Platforms:

- Social media platforms provide a platform for public speaking through posts, live videos, stories, and audio content. They allow you to share your thoughts, expertise, and insights with your followers and engage in conversations with a broader audience.

7. Online Learning Platforms:

- Online learning platforms offer opportunities for public speaking through educational courses, workshops, and training programs. Platforms enable you to create and deliver online courses on topics of your expertise, reaching learners worldwide.

8. Virtual Reality (VR) Platforms:

- Virtual reality platforms provide immersive experiences for public speaking and presentations in virtual environments. Platforms offer virtual meeting spaces where you can deliver speeches, host meetings, or collaborate with others in a 3D virtual environment.

9. Professional Networking Platforms:

- Professional networking platforms offer opportunities for public speaking through virtual events, webinars, and discussions with industry professionals. Platforms provide spaces for hosting and participating in professional conversations, sharing insights, and establishing thought leadership in your field.

10. Online Communities and Forums:

- Online communities and forums offer opportunities for public speaking through discussions, forums, and online groups. Platforms enable you to engage with communities of like-minded individuals, share your expertise, and participate in conversations on topics relevant to your interests or industry.

Live Streaming and Virtual Presentations

In the digital age, live streaming and virtual presentations have become essential tools for public speaking, enabling speakers to reach global audiences and engage with them in real-time. Here's a practical guide on how to effectively leverage live streaming and virtual presentations for public speaking:

1. **Choose the Right Platform:**
   - Select a reliable live streaming platform or virtual event software that meets your needs and audience preferences. Consider factors such as audience size, features (e.g., chat, Q&A, polls), ease of use, and compatibility with your content and branding.

2. **Plan Your Presentation:**
   - Plan your presentation carefully, taking into account the unique characteristics of virtual audiences. Structure your content in a way that captures and maintains audience attention, considering factors such as screen fatigue and distractions.

3. **Prepare Your Technology:**
   - Test your equipment, internet connection, and software well in advance to ensure smooth and seamless delivery. Consider using a high-quality webcam, microphone, and lighting setup to enhance your video and audio quality.

4. **Engage Your Audience:**
   - Actively engage your audience throughout the presentation to keep them involved and attentive. Encourage participation through interactive elements such as live chat, polls, and Q&A sessions. Address questions and comments in real-time to foster a sense of connection and community.

5. **Use Visual Aids Effectively:**
   - Incorporate visual aids, such as slides, graphics, or videos, to enhance your presentation and reinforce key points. Keep visuals clear, concise, and visually appealing, avoiding clutter or distractions that may detract from your message.

6. **Practice Your Delivery:**
   - Rehearse your presentation multiple times to familiarize yourself with the content and delivery. Practice speaking clearly, confidently, and at a comfortable pace, paying attention to your tone, gestures, and facial expressions.

7. Optimize for Interaction:

- Design your presentation with interactivity in mind, creating opportunities for audience engagement and participation. Encourage viewers to ask questions, share insights, or participate in activities that facilitate learning and interaction.

8. Manage Technical Issues Proactively:

- Anticipate and prepare for technical issues that may arise during the live stream, such as audio/video glitches, internet disruptions, or software malfunctions. Have a backup plan in place and troubleshoot any issues promptly to minimize disruptions to the presentation.

9. Promote Your Event:

- Promote your live stream or virtual presentation in advance to attract and inform potential attendees. Use email newsletters, social media posts, and online advertisements to build anticipation and generate interest in your event.

10. Follow Up After the Event:

- Follow up with attendees after the event to thank them for their participation and provide additional resources or materials related to the presentation. Solicit feedback to gain insights into audience satisfaction and identify areas for improvement in future presentations.

11. Continuously Improve:

- Review recordings of your live streams or virtual presentations to evaluate your performance and identify areas for improvement. Solicit feedback from attendees and peers to gain insights into what worked well and what could be enhanced in future presentations.

12. Stay Engaged with Your Audience:

- Maintain ongoing engagement with your audience beyond the live stream or virtual event. Continue the conversation on social media, host follow-up discussions or webinars, and provide valuable content that reinforces your expertise and keeps your audience engaged over time.

Podcasting and Video Content Creation

In the digital age, podcasting and video content creation have emerged as powerful mediums for public speaking, enabling speakers to reach and engage with diverse audiences worldwide. Here's a practical guide on how to effectively leverage podcasting and video content creation for public speaking:

1. **Define Your Niche and Audience:**
   - Identify your niche and target audience for your podcast or video content. Determine the topics, themes, and formats that align with your expertise and resonate with your audience's interests and needs.

2. **Choose Your Format:**
   - Decide on the format of your podcast or video content, whether it's solo episodes, interviews, panel discussions, tutorials, or vlogs. Choose a format that best suits your content goals, speaking style, and audience preferences.

3. **Plan Your Content:**
   - Plan your podcast episodes or video content carefully, outlining the topics, structure, and key points you want to cover in each episode or video. Consider creating a content calendar to stay organized and ensure consistency in your publishing schedule.

4. **Invest in Quality Equipment:**
   - Invest in quality recording equipment, including microphones, cameras, lighting, and editing software, to ensure professional-quality audio and video production. Consider your budget and technical requirements when choosing equipment that meets your needs.

5. **Create Compelling Content:**
   - Create compelling and valuable content that educates, entertains, or inspires your audience. Offer unique insights, perspectives, and expertise that differentiate your podcast or video content from others in your niche. Focus on providing actionable takeaways and practical advice that resonate with your audience.

6. **Master Your Delivery:**

- Master your delivery and presentation skills to engage and captivate your audience. Speak clearly, confidently, and authentically, using conversational language and tone to connect with listeners or viewers. Pay attention to pacing, intonation, and emphasis to keep the audience engaged throughout your content.

7. Optimize for SEO and Discovery:
   - Optimize your podcast or video content for search engine optimization (SEO) and discoverability to attract new listeners or viewers. Use relevant keywords, titles, and descriptions in your podcast episodes or video titles to improve visibility and ranking in search results.

8. Promote Your Content:
   - Promote your podcast or video content across multiple channels to expand your reach and attract a larger audience. Utilize social media, email newsletters, guest appearances, and collaboration opportunities to increase awareness and drive traffic to your content.

9. Engage with Your Audience:
   - Engage with your audience actively by encouraging feedback, comments, and interactions on your podcast episodes or video content. Respond to listener or viewer questions, comments, and feedback to foster a sense of community and connection with your audience.

10. Collaborate with Guests and Partners:
   - Collaborate with guests, influencers, or industry experts to add variety and depth to your podcast or video content. Invite guest speakers for interviews, panel discussions, or co-hosting opportunities to provide diverse perspectives and insights to your audience.

11. Consistently Publish Quality Content:
   - Consistently publish high-quality content on a regular basis to maintain momentum and grow your audience over time. Stick to a consistent publishing schedule and deliver valuable content that keeps your audience engaged and coming back for more.

12. Monitor Performance and Iterate:

- Monitor the performance of your podcast episodes or video content by tracking metrics such as downloads, views, engagement, and subscriber growth. Use analytics and feedback to identify trends, understand audience preferences, and iterate on your content strategy to improve over time.

Navigating Social Media as a Public Speaker

Navigating social media as a public speaker is crucial in the digital age to connect with your audience, build your brand, and promote your speaking engagements. Here's a practical guide on how to effectively leverage social media as a public speaker:

1. **Choose the Right Platforms:**
   - Identify the social media platforms that align with your target audience and speaking goals. Focus on platforms where your audience is most active and engaged.

2. **Create a Professional Profile:**
   - Create a professional profile on each social media platform, using a consistent username, profile photo, and bio that reflect your identity as a public speaker. Highlight your expertise, experience, and speaking topics in your bio to attract followers and showcase your credibility.

3. **Share Valuable Content:**
   - Share valuable and relevant content on your social media channels that resonates with your audience's interests and needs. Provide insights, tips, and resources related to your speaking topics, and share behind-the-scenes glimpses of your speaking engagements, preparation process, or personal experiences.

4. **Engage with Your Audience:**
   - Actively engage with your audience on social media by responding to comments, messages, and mentions promptly. Foster meaningful conversations, ask questions, and encourage interaction to build relationships and rapport with your followers.

5. **Promote Your Speaking Engagements:**

- Use social media to promote your upcoming speaking engagements, workshops, or events. Create eye-catching graphics, videos, or event pages to announce your speaking engagements, share event details, and encourage attendance from your followers.

6. Share Testimonials and Feedback:

- Share testimonials, reviews, and feedback from past speaking engagements to showcase your expertise and credibility as a speaker. Highlight positive comments, endorsements, or reviews from event organizers, attendees, or clients to build trust and social proof.

7. Network with Peers and Influencers:

- Connect with other speakers, influencers, and industry professionals on social media to expand your network and visibility within your niche. Engage in conversations, share each other's content, and collaborate on projects or events to leverage mutual support and exposure.

8. Provide Value to Your Audience:

- Provide value to your social media audience by sharing informative, entertaining, or inspirational content that enriches their lives or solves their problems. Offer actionable advice, share success stories, and address common challenges or questions related to your speaking topics.

9. Stay Consistent and Authentic:

- Maintain a consistent presence on social media by posting regularly and sharing content that reflects your personality, values, and brand as a speaker. Be authentic, genuine, and transparent in your interactions to build trust and authenticity with your audience.

10. Use Hashtags and Keywords:

- Utilize relevant hashtags and keywords in your social media posts to increase visibility and reach a wider audience. Research popular hashtags and keywords related to your speaking topics or industry and incorporate them strategically into your content.

11. Measure Your Impact:

- Track and measure the impact of your social media efforts using analytics tools provided by each platform. Monitor metrics such as follower growth, engagement rates, website traffic, and conversion rates to assess the effectiveness of your social media strategy and make data-driven decisions for optimization.

12. Stay Up-to-Date with Trends:
- Stay informed about social media trends, updates, and best practices to adapt your strategy and stay ahead of the curve. Experiment with new features, formats, or trends on social media to keep your content fresh, relevant, and engaging for your audience.

Staying Relevant in the Evolving Digital Landscape

Staying relevant in the evolving digital landscape as a public speaker is essential to maintain your audience's engagement and grow your influence over time. Here's a practical guide on how to stay relevant in the digital age:

1. Stay Informed About Industry Trends:
- Keep yourself updated on industry trends, emerging technologies, and evolving audience preferences related to public speaking. Follow thought leaders, attend conferences, read industry publications, and participate in online communities to stay informed and adapt your approach accordingly.

2. Embrace Digital Tools and Platforms:
- Embrace digital tools, platforms, and technologies that facilitate public speaking and audience engagement in the digital age. Experiment with new tools for content creation, virtual presentations, live streaming, podcasting, or social media marketing to expand your reach and relevance.

3. Adapt to Changing Audience Preferences:
- Adapt your content, delivery style, and presentation format to align with changing audience preferences and behaviors in the digital landscape. Cater to shorter attention spans, embrace multimedia

formats, and provide interactive and engaging experiences to capture and retain audience interest.

4. Offer Value-Driven Content:
   - Focus on providing value-driven content that addresses your audience's needs, challenges, and interests. Offer actionable insights, practical advice, and relevant information that helps your audience solve problems, achieve goals, or gain new perspectives.

5. Engage with Your Audience Consistently:
   - Maintain consistent engagement with your audience across digital channels by sharing regular updates, responding to comments, and fostering meaningful interactions. Actively listen to your audience's feedback, questions, and concerns, and incorporate their input into your content and strategy.

6. Stay Authentic and Genuine:
   - Maintain authenticity and genuineness in your public speaking endeavors to build trust and credibility with your audience. Share personal stories, experiences, and vulnerabilities to connect on a deeper level with your audience and demonstrate authenticity in your communication.

7. Collaborate and Network with Peers:
   - Collaborate and network with other public speakers, influencers, and industry professionals to stay connected and relevant in the digital landscape. Seek opportunities for partnerships, joint ventures, or co-creation of content to leverage each other's expertise and reach a broader audience.

8. Continuously Improve Your Skills:
   - Invest in continuous learning and skill development to enhance your public speaking abilities and adapt to the evolving digital landscape. Attend workshops, courses, or coaching sessions to refine your presentation skills, storytelling techniques, and audience engagement strategies.

9. Monitor and Analyze Performance Metrics:

- Monitor and analyze performance metrics related to your public speaking efforts, including audience engagement, reach, feedback, and conversion rates. Use data-driven insights to assess the effectiveness of your strategies and make informed decisions for optimization and improvement.

10. **Stay Resilient and Flexible:**
   - Stay resilient and flexible in navigating challenges and changes in the digital landscape. Embrace experimentation, innovation, and adaptation to overcome obstacles and seize new opportunities for growth and relevance as a public speaker.

Chapter 19
Public Speaking
Success Stories

Profiles of Successful Public Speakers

Profile 1: The Storyteller

Background: Coming from a diverse background in the arts and communication, this speaker has honed the craft of storytelling to captivate audiences. With a degree in literature and a background in theater, they bring stories to life in a way that resonates with listeners on an emotional level.

Key Skills:

Emotional Intelligence: The ability to read the room and adapt the tone and pace of the story accordingly.
Imaginative Storytelling: Uses vivid imagery and personal anecdotes to create a connection with the audience.
Engaging Presence: Combines body language and vocal variety to keep the audience engaged and invested in the story.

Success Strategies:

 - Crafting each speech as a journey, with a clear beginning, middle, and end, that takes the audience on an emotional and intellectual ride.
 - Incorporating lessons and insights into stories, making complex ideas accessible and memorable.
 - Practicing active listening during Q&A sessions to respond thoughtfully and create a dialogue with the audience.

Profile 2: The Expert

Background: With a PhD in behavioral psychology and years of research experience, this speaker brings a depth of knowledge to topics related to human behavior and motivation. They translate complex concepts into understandable language, making them a sought-after speaker for conferences, workshops, and corporate events.

Key Skills:

Deep Subject Matter Expertise: Possesses a wealth of knowledge and continuously stays updated with the latest research.

Clarity and Precision: Breaks down complex ideas into clear, concise statements that are easily understood.
Audience Engagement: Uses interactive elements like Q&A sessions, live polls, and practical demonstrations to involve the audience.

Success Strategies:

- Tailoring presentations to the audience's level of understanding and interest.
- Using data and evidence to back up claims, adding credibility to their speeches.
- Encouraging audience participation to foster a sense of involvement and investment.

Profile 3: The Inspirational Leader

Background: With a history of overcoming personal and professional challenges, this speaker focuses on themes of resilience, leadership, and personal growth. They have led teams through significant changes and challenges, emerging stronger and more united.

Key Skills:

Powerful Personal Narratives: Shares personal experiences of overcoming adversity to inspire others.
Motivational Techniques: Understands how to motivate different types of people and tailors messages to resonate with diverse audiences.
Charismatic Delivery: Captivates the audience with a dynamic presence and powerful delivery that commands attention.

Success Strategies:

- Focusing on the positive outcomes of facing and overcoming challenges.
- Providing actionable advice and strategies that audience members can apply in their own lives.
- Creating a sense of community and shared purpose within the audience, making each individual feel part of something larger.

Each of these profiles represents a unique approach to public speaking, emphasizing different skills and strategies that contribute to success. Whether through the power of storytelling, the sharing of expert knowledge, or inspiring through personal experiences, these speakers connect with their audiences in meaningful ways, leaving lasting impressions and delivering valuable insights.

Learning from Notable Speeches in History

Speech 1: The Call for Unity

Context: Amidst a period of significant societal division, a leader delivers a speech that aims to bridge gaps and foster a sense of unity among diverse groups.

Key Elements:

Empathy and Understanding: The speaker starts by acknowledging the differences and grievances that exist, showing a deep understanding of the various perspectives.
Common Ground: Identifies shared values and goals that all parties can agree on, using these as a foundation for building unity.
Vision for the Future: Paints a vivid picture of what a unified future could look like, emphasizing the benefits for all involved.

Lessons Learned:

- The power of empathy in communication to build bridges.
- The importance of focusing on common goals and values to unite diverse groups.
- The effectiveness of a compelling vision to motivate and inspire action.

Speech 2: The Innovation Imperative

Context: During a technological conference, an inventor unveils a groundbreaking technology that has the potential to change the world, addressing the importance of continuous innovation.

Key Elements:

Highlighting the Problem: Begins by detailing the current challenges and limitations faced by society, setting the stage for the solution.
Introducing the Solution: Describes the new technology in simple terms, focusing on its benefits and potential to address the aforementioned problems.
Call to Action: Encourages stakeholders to embrace change and innovation, outlining steps for involvement and adoption.

Lessons Learned:

 - The importance of clearly defining problems before presenting solutions.
 - Making complex ideas accessible to a broad audience.
 - The role of a strong call to action to drive engagement and commitment.

Speech 3: The Environmental Pledge

Context: At an international environmental summit, an environmentalist delivers a passionate speech about the urgent need for action on climate change, proposing a global initiative.

Key Elements:

Urgency and Impact: Details the dire consequences of inaction, using vivid imagery and data to highlight the severity of the situation.
Responsibility and Hope: Balances the urgency with a message of hope, emphasizing human responsibility and the ability to make a difference.
Global Collaboration: Calls for a united global effort, outlining a plan for collaboration across countries, industries, and communities.

Lessons Learned:

 - The use of compelling evidence and imagery to convey urgency.
 - Balancing dire warnings with a positive message of hope and possibility.

- The importance of calling for collective action in addressing global challenges.

General Principles for Memorable Speeches

Connect on an Emotional Level: Whether through storytelling, shared values, or highlighting common challenges, emotional connection is key.
Clarity and Simplicity: Conveying complex ideas in simple, understandable terms broadens impact.
Strong Openings and Closings: Begin with a statement that grabs attention and conclude with a memorable call to action.
Authenticity: Genuine passion and belief in the message resonate more deeply with audiences.

These examples and lessons underline the universal principles of effective public speaking: connecting with the audience, clearly communicating ideas, and inspiring action. These strategies, when employed thoughtfully, can make speeches powerful tools for change and influence.

Inspirational Journeys of Overcoming Public Speaking Challenges

Journey 1: The Shy Innovator

Background: A tech genius, inherently introverted and reserved, found themselves at a crossroads when their groundbreaking invention demanded public attention. Initially, the thought of presenting in front of an audience caused sleepless nights and intense anxiety.

Overcoming the Challenge:

Step by Step Exposure: They started by sharing their ideas in small, informal groups, gradually increasing the audience size as confidence grew.

Seeking Mentorship: A seasoned public speaker mentored them, providing tips on storytelling, engaging the audience, and managing nerves.

Embracing Technology: Utilized presentation software and virtual reality simulations to practice and hone public speaking skills in a controlled environment.

Outcome: Became a celebrated speaker known for captivating presentations on innovation, often highlighted by personal anecdotes of overcoming shyness, which inspired many in the tech community.

Journey 2: The Accidental Leader

Background: Thrust into a leadership role during a crisis within their community organization, this individual was petrified at the thought of leading meetings and speaking publicly. Their initial attempts were marked by stuttering, forgetfulness, and physical symptoms of stress.

Overcoming the Challenge:

Embracing Vulnerability: Openly shared their fears with the team, which led to an outpouring of support and understanding, reducing the pressure to appear perfect.

Practical Skills Training: Attended workshops on public speaking, leadership, and stress management, applying learned techniques to improve gradually.

Routine Practice: Implemented regular practice sessions, both alone and in front of trusted friends, to build confidence and receive constructive feedback.

Outcome: Transformed into a confident leader who inspired their team through authentic and heartfelt communication, leading the organization to new heights.

Journey 3: The Reluctant Advocate

Background: After personally experiencing a life-changing event, this individual felt a burning need to advocate for change. However, their deep-rooted fear of public speaking made the prospect of advocacy seem impossible.

Overcoming the Challenge:

Finding Passion: The strong desire to see change became the catalyst for overcoming their speaking fears, proving that passion can drive one beyond comfort zones.
Community Engagement: Started by writing about their cause, gradually moving to speaking at small community gatherings before eventually addressing larger audiences.
Professional Guidance: Worked with a speech therapist and a public speaking coach to tackle both the physical and psychological aspects of speaking anxiety.

Outcome: Emerged as a powerful voice for their cause, using their story to connect deeply with others and effect change, demonstrating that even the most reluctant speaker can become a force for good.

Key Takeaways

These journeys illustrate that overcoming public speaking challenges often involves a combination of personal growth, skill development, and the support of others. Whether it's through incremental exposure, embracing vulnerability, or finding a passion that drives you, the path to becoming a confident speaker is as diverse as the individuals who walk it. Importantly, these stories remind us that the fear of public speaking is surmountable, and beyond it lies the opportunity to inspire, lead, and make an impact.

Celebrating Diverse Voices in Public Speaking

Speaker 1: The Cultural Bridge-Builder

Background: Born into a multicultural family and having lived in several countries, this speaker brings a wealth of cross-cultural experiences to the table. They have navigated the complexities of maintaining their cultural identity while adapting to new environments, languages, and customs.

Contribution: Through engaging talks and workshops, the Cultural Bridge-Builder emphasizes the value of cultural diversity, the richness it brings to societies, and the importance of cross-cultural communication. They share stories of integration, identity, and intercultural understanding, offering insights into how diverse cultural backgrounds can foster creativity, innovation, and empathy.

Impact: Audiences leave with a deeper appreciation for cultural diversity and practical strategies for improving communication and collaboration in multicultural settings. This speaker inspires businesses, educational institutions, and community organizations to embrace inclusivity and leverage the strengths of their diverse teams.

Speaker 2: The Advocate for Inclusivity

Background: Having faced and overcome significant barriers due to a physical disability, this speaker has become a powerful advocate for inclusivity and accessibility. Their personal journey highlights the challenges and triumphs of living with a disability, driving them to champion the rights and potential of people with disabilities.

Contribution: The Advocate for Inclusivity delivers compelling narratives about navigating a world not always designed for accessibility, shining a light on the importance of inclusive practices and policies. They share innovative solutions for creating accessible environments and advocate for the inclusion of people with disabilities in all areas of public and private life.

Impact: Their talks not only raise awareness about the importance of accessibility and inclusivity but also challenge stereotypes about disability. Organizations are encouraged to adopt more inclusive practices, and individuals are inspired to advocate for change in their communities.

Speaker 3: The Environmental Visionary

Background: Coming from a region severely affected by environmental degradation, this speaker has witnessed firsthand the impacts of climate change on vulnerable communities. Their passion for environmental justice has led them to become a spokesperson for sustainable living and conservation efforts.

Contribution: The Environmental Visionary uses their platform to highlight the interconnectedness of human and environmental health, advocating for policies and practices that promote sustainability. Through vivid storytelling and sharing innovative approaches to conservation, they bring attention to the urgent need for action on climate change, especially as it affects underrepresented and vulnerable populations.

Impact: Their speeches inspire individuals and organizations to consider the environmental impact of their actions and to take meaningful steps toward sustainability. They bring a unique perspective on how climate change disproportionately affects certain communities, emphasizing the need for inclusive solutions that consider the needs of all, especially the most vulnerable.

The Collective Impact

These speakers exemplify the power of diverse voices in enriching public dialogue and sparking change. Their unique perspectives and experiences contribute to a more nuanced understanding of complex issues, fostering empathy, inclusivity, and action among their audiences. Celebrating and amplifying diverse voices in public speaking not only reflects the multifaceted nature of society but also drives progress by including all voices in the conversation.

Personal Reflections on Public Speaking Triumphs

Reflection 1: Embracing Vulnerability

Journey: Initially, the prospect of public speaking filled me with dread. My hands would shake, and my voice would quiver at the thought of standing in front of an audience. I believed that to be a good speaker, I had to project a façade of unshakeable confidence and perfection. However, this pursuit of perfection only magnified my fear.

Triumph: My perspective shifted when I attended a workshop that emphasized the power of vulnerability in public speaking. I learned that audiences connect more deeply with speakers who show their true selves, including their imperfections. In my next speech, I shared a personal story of failure and how it led to unexpected growth. The audience's warm and engaged response was a revelation.

Lesson: Embracing vulnerability transformed my approach to public speaking. It taught me that authenticity resonates more than perfection. This realization not only alleviated my fear but also made my speeches more impactful and relatable.

Reflection 2: Turning Anxiety into Energy

Journey: For me, public speaking anxiety was a physical battle. My heart would race, and my mind would fog up under stress. Despite understanding my topics inside and out, translating that knowledge into a compelling presentation seemed an insurmountable task. I was on the verge of letting my anxiety define my capabilities.

Triumph: The turning point came when a mentor introduced me to techniques for channeling nervous energy into enthusiasm for my subject. I started incorporating physical exercises to manage my stress and practiced mindfulness to stay focused. By reframing my anxiety as excitement, I was able to harness that energy positively during my speeches.

Lesson: The experience taught me that anxiety doesn't have to be a barrier. Instead, it can be a powerful force that, when directed properly, enhances my speaking performance. This mindset shift has been crucial in not just surviving but thriving in public speaking scenarios.

Reflection 3: The Journey from Solitude to the Stage

Journey: As someone who preferred solitude, the idea of engaging with an audience was foreign to me. My comfort zone was behind the scenes, where I felt my contributions were best made. However, a passion for a cause I deeply cared about pushed me out of the shadows.

I realized that if I wanted to make a real difference, I needed to share my message directly.

Triumph: My first few attempts were clumsy, but each experience was a stepping stone. I sought feedback, refined my approach, and gradually found my voice. The real triumph came when I spoke at a large event about my cause, feeling an exhilarating mix of fear and excitement. The audience's response—cheers, applause, and engaging questions—was beyond anything I had imagined.

Lesson: This journey taught me the power of passion as a motivator for overcoming personal limitations. By focusing on the message I wanted to convey and the change I hoped to inspire, public speaking became not just a task, but a mission. It transformed my understanding of influence and the role each of us can play in shaping the world.

These reflections underscore that triumphs in public speaking are as much about personal growth as they are about the techniques and strategies employed. They highlight the journey of overcoming internal barriers, the transformation that occurs through perseverance, and the profound impact of sharing one's voice with the world.